"This book tackles, head-on, a significant, high-priority clinical problem that many patients and therapists dread and avoid. It offers cool, clear thinking, immensely helpful to both patient and clinician, and dozens of practical, down-to-earth suggestions. A brave and extremely sensible book from which I learned quite a bit. I am delighted to have this 'weapon' in my armory when I work with suicidal patients."

—Jacqueline B. Persons, Ph.D., Director,
Center for Cognitive Therapy, Oakland, California

"Tom Ellis and Cory Newman have written a wonderful book. The writing is clear and the message is important. The authors are gifted clinicians, and their empathic concern for depressed and suicidal people comes through on every page. Anyone who has contemplated suicide and anyone with a suicidal loved one will profit from the straightforward and helpful suggestions in this book."

—Danny Wedding, Ph.D., M.P.H., Director,
Missouri Institute of Mental Health

"In the best tradition of giving psychology away, this easy-to-read book can help suicidal people understand their suffering while they take charge of their own healing. Some readers will need additional professional help, but all will benefit from *Choosing to Live*'s message of hope and reassurance that suicide is not the answer."

—Paul G. Quinnett, author of
Suicide: The Forever Decision

CHOOSING TO Live

HOW TO

DEFEAT SUICIDE

THROUGH

COGNITIVE THERAPY

THOMAS E. ELLIS, PSY.D.

CORY F. NEWMAN, PH.D.

FOREWORD BY

AARON T. BECK, M.D.

NEW HARBINGER

PUBLICATIONS, INC.

Publisher's Note

This publication is designed to provide accurate and authoritative information in regard to the subject matter covered. It is sold with the understanding that the publisher is not engaged in rendering pyschological, financial, legal, or other professional services. If expert assistance or counseling is needed, the services of a competent professional should be sought.

Copyright © 1996 Thomas E. Ellis, Psy.D., and Cory F. Newman, Ph.D.
        New Harbinger Publications, Inc.
        5674 Shattuck Avenue
        Oakland, CA 94609

Cover design by Poulson/Gluck Design.
Text design by Tracy Marie Powell.

Distributed in U.S.A. primarily by Publishers Group West; in Canada by Raincoast Books; in Great Britain by Airlift Book Company, Ltd.; in South Africa by Real Books, Ltd.; in Australia by Boobook; in New Zealand by Tandem Press.

Library of Congress Catalog Card Number: 96-67944

ISBN 1-57224-056-3 paperback

Printed in Canada.

First printing 1996, 6,000 copies

For my wife, Clare, and son, Taylor, who remind me that reasons for living are always there, if you look for them.

—T.E.

For Rob, whom I wish I had gotten to know before he left this world.

—C.N.

"Difficulties lie in our habits of thought rather than in the nature of things."

—Andre Tardieu

"It is no easy thing for a principle to become a man's own, unless each day he maintain it and hear it maintained, as well as work it out in life."

—Epictetus

Contents

Part IV: Appendix

What Warning Signs Should I Look For? • Is This My Fault?
• She's Threatening to Kill Herself: What Should I Do? • What
Can I Do if He Refuses to Be Helped? • What Do I Do if I Feel
I'm Being Manipulated by the Suicide Threats? • What Should
I Be Careful *Not* to Do?

Books • Organizations

List of Exercises

Foreword

Of all the forms of human suffering, few compare with the pain that leads some to think of suicide as a means of relief. Yet an enormous amount of clinical experience and a large body of research show that this suffering can be alleviated by addressing its causes. Studies have shown that much of the pain and, consequently, the desire to stop living, is based on the suicidal person's desperate view of his or her plight. Suicidal people perceive their problems as towering over them, casting an all-encompassing shadow. They regard themselves as inadequate, undesirable, or irremediably ill. As they look ahead they can see only frustration and continuing pain.

People who regard suicide as the only way out sometimes feel abandoned or alone after the loss of a close relationship. They think, "I will never find love again." Others regard themselves as abysmal failures after a reversal in their academic or career pursuits and think, "I am a shameful loser who can never face anyone again." They have a sort of tunnel vision that focuses all of their attention on their losses, setbacks, and the discouraging meanings they attribute to them.

But there is light at the end of the tunnel. Drs. Ellis and Newman provide illumination to guide people in combating the negative thinking that contributes to their pain and suicidal wishes. The approach in *Choosing to Live: How to Defeat Suicide through Cognitive Therapy* rests on a solid foundation of research that pinpoints the causes of depression and suicidality and aims toward relief from emotional pain and suffering. Application of the principles outlined by Drs. Ellis and Newman has helped to reverse the despair that depressed individuals experience, giving them hope for a more fulfilling existence.

When therapists and loved ones encourage a deeply depressed person to choose life over death, they often encounter someone who feels it is too difficult and painful to go on. Such a person needs support and inspiration, but this is not enough. The deeply depressed person also needs a set of *methods* to use in order to rebuild his or her sense of purpose, meaning, and skills in dealing with what life has to offer. *Choosing to Live* focuses on both goals—providing inspiration *and* instruction.

The authors' empathy for the plight of suicidal persons and their loved ones is apparent throughout the book. They speak directly to the hopelessness, frustration, and loss that often fuel a person's wish to die, and to the fear and dismay that characterize the reactions of loved ones. Further, the authors understand that most suicidal people have mixed emotions about living and dying and find themselves in a terrible quandary. Suicidal people want to end their pain and suffering; but they are almost entirely convinced that the only way to do this is to end life itself, since nothing less drastic seems to have worked. Still, if they could just find another way, they would choose not to die, but rather to live a better life—but how? The authors present the strategies and philosophies of *cognitive therapy*—a treatment that has been proven effective in the treatment of depression and other disorders—to help people answer this question.

In reading through the pages of *Choosing to Live*, one realizes that suicidal feelings are nothing to be ashamed of, as they are neither rare nor signs of "craziness." However, people unnecessarily take their lives every day, partly because of their hesitancy to ask for help and partly because they believe there is nothing left to do that will make things better. The cognitive therapy approach addresses both of these problems.

By reading this book, you will gain valuable assistance, even if you are hesitant to discuss suicidal feelings openly with others (although the authors duly note that this book is not a *substitute* for professional treatment). You also will learn that remaining alive is not merely an exercise in hanging on, gritting your teeth, and accepting all manner of emotional pain and suffering day after day with no end in sight. Rather, you will be instructed in methods that communicate an appreciation for yourself and your life and that help make life a more appealing option. You will become familiar with such important skills as (1) being aware of the things you say to yourself automatically—the sorts of thoughts that drag you down, punish you, and make you feel hopeless; (2) changing those thoughts so that you give yourself and your life situation a fair, objective evaluation, free of undue, oppressive negativity; (3) becoming adept at recognizing your strengths and resources as a person; (4) improving the quality of your communication and general ways of relating with other people who matter to you; (5) solving problems, including the big ones that have dominated your life, as well as the everyday problems that otherwise wear you down; (6) dealing with losses you have suffered, with an eye toward new aspirations and relationships in the future; and (7) using your time so that you get more enjoyment and meaning out of each day. The authors serve as your compassionate coaches, helping you to apply these strategies through a series of inventive and highly useful exercises.

If you are someone who is trying to understand and cope with the suicidality of a loved one, this book also provides valuable insights into how to relate to a suicidal person in mutually beneficial ways (while also giving guidance on enlisting the help of a mental health professional).

This valuable book takes the mystery and stigma out of suicidality. It provides a wealth of ideas for understanding and counteracting painful emotions and negative views of yourself, your life, and your future. It not only inspires, but also provides the means by which to move from the darkness of self-destruction to a better life.

Aaron T. Beck, M.D., President
The Beck Institute for Cognitive Therapy and Research
University Professor Emeritus of Psychiatry
University of Pennsylvania

Introduction

This book is for people who have considered suicide and for those who love them. It is for those whose emotional or physical pain has cast such a shadow over their lives that death has begun to seem alluring. It is for the individual whose therapist has suggested it to assist in the healing process or for the bookstore browser surprised to find a title that hits so close to home.

The idea for this book evolved from an utterance by a patient who, in trying to get across what it was like to be suicidal, exclaimed, "It's like I want to be dead, but not forever!" That statement captures the essence of the stormy, often contradictory, feelings that people experience when thoughts of self-destruction enter their minds. The idea of deliverance from life's trials and tribulations can indeed be seductive. But death is a drastic—and very permanent—"solution."

By picking up this book, you have shown that you, too, have mixed feelings about suicide: You've considered it seriously enough that it is an issue in your life, but you're still looking for a less extreme road to a better place for yourself.

*Cognitive therapy** is a modern, tested way of improving peoples lives by changing how they view the world and interpret what happens to them. It has helped thousands of people reduce emotional distress and develop more effective coping behaviors. Scientific studies have confirmed that cog-

---

* The term *cognitive therapy* has appeared in the literature to refer specifically to Dr. Aaron T. Beck's therapeutic formulations and generically to refer to various cognitive-oriented therapies. These include Beck's Cognitive Therapy, Albert Ellis's Rational-Emotive Behavior Therapy, cognitive-behavior therapy, and others. In this book, the term cognitive therapy is used in the generic sense.

nitive therapy is effective in treating a variety of disorders, whether characterized primarily by depression, anxiety, panic, disordered eating patterns, substance abuse, or relationship difficulties.

A number of self-help books based on cognitive procedures have appeared in recent years, but none are specifically for persons with suicidal thoughts and behaviors. This has not been for lack of evidence that cognitive therapy might benefit this group. Studies have shown that suicidal people often have certain distinguishing characteristics (such as black-and-white thinking and deficient problem-solving skills) that are amenable to cognitively focused therapies. It is the purpose of our book to fill this gap.

How to Use This Book

Although this book is designed to be read and applied by you, the reader, it is not intended as a substitute for professional help. We recommend that you use it in the context of a working relationship with a qualified therapist (see the next section, "Do You Need Professional Assistance?").

Reading the material is only one step in your efforts to improve your life. You will need to read and reread many passages, and we hope that you will underline helpful passages and make notes in the margins. As you read, you will find many written exercises and suggestions for what you can *do* that will make changes become a reality for you. By all means, *do the exercises.* You will understand the importance of practice exercises if you compare your self-change efforts to improving at a sport or learning to play a musical instrument—reading can help you along, but the only way you'll become good is to practice, practice, practice!

As with any such endeavor, its important to allow yourself to be a beginner—stumbling, making mistakes, even getting discouraged occasionally are all parts of the process. Remember, just as you wouldn't expect to be able to play a concerto after your first week at the piano, you also shouldn't expect to "get" cognitive therapy with your first glance at this book. If your first efforts don't produce dramatic results, give yourself time and understanding; and by all means, seek help and encouragement from a trusted friend or a therapist.

Do You Need Professional Assistance?

If you meet any of the criteria listed below, we recommend that you seek professional help immediately.

- You have planned your suicide and have the means available to carry it out.

- You are suicidal and currently using alcohol or other drugs to excess.

- You are unable to eat or sleep.

- You see this book as your last resort and have decided to kill yourself if it doesn't help.

- You are hearing voices or in any other way having difficulty knowing what is real and what is not.

- You are having flashbacks to prior traumatic experiences.

- You are having difficulty accounting for blocks of time.

- You are both severely depressed and experiencing severe anxiety.

These symptoms are signs of urgent psychological crises that require immediate, sometimes medical, intervention. All respond to treatment. Once these more urgent, disruptive symptoms are being taken care of, you will be in a much better position to benefit from the strategies described here.

Message to Parents and Other Loved Ones

If you are a parent who is reading this because of concerns about your adolescent son or daughter, you will notice that our book focuses primarily on adults. This is not because of any lack of concern over the significant increase in recent years in adolescent suicides and suicide attempts, but simply a reflection of the adult focus in our clinical training and practices. While most of the principles and strategies in this book apply equally well to teenagers and adults, teens do differ from adults in some important ways. Therefore, in addition to this volume, you might wish to read teen-specific material such as Sol Gordon's *When Living Hurts* and recommend it to your child. We also recommend that you discuss concerns about your son or daughter with a mental health professional who has specialty training in working with adolescents and their families.

For readers who are concerned about an adult friend or relative, we suggest that you consult Appendix A, "A Guide for Concerned Friends and Family Members." You probably will also find much of the rest of the book (especially the first three chapters) to be helpful to you in better understanding what your friend or family member is experiencing and what you might be able to do to help.

Note to Clinicians

We recommend that this book be used in the context of a therapeutic relationship. We recognize that many self-help books, although read with initial enthusiasm, are quickly forgotten by readers. This, we believe, is for much the same reasons that nonadherence to therapy homework assignments is so common: Change is hard, complicated work, and the dysfunctional cognitions that interfere with homework assignments are often the very ones that cause problems in the first place. However, as is also the case with therapy homework, persistence and problem solving generally increase adherence, and the benefits derived are well worth the effort. We assume that most patients sincerely want to get better, and we look to you, the professional, to assist readers in their efforts to take ideas from our book and put them to work to improve their lives.

Although the framework of this book is cognitive/behavioral, the therapeutic strategies described herein are compatible with most therapy orientations. For clinicians interested in learning more about the cognitive model of suicidality and cognitive-behavioral treatment of suicidal patients, we recommend Ellis (1986, 1987); Fremouw, dePerczel, and Ellis (1990); Layden, Newman, Freeman, and Morse (1993); Linehan (1993); and Freeman and Reinecke (1993). In addition, we strongly urge the interested clinician to study Aaron Beck's cognitive conceptualization of depression (Beck 1967; Beck et al. 1979) and Albert Ellis's expositions on Rational-Emotive Behavior Therapy (REBT; Ellis 1994).

Finally, we would be remiss not to acknowledge our debt to the pioneering work of Marsha Linehan (1993) in the understanding and treatment of suicidal individuals. Although her work focuses primarily on persons with borderline personality disorder, most of it can be generalized to other groups of suicidal patients. In particular, we have been influenced by her emphasis on a multidimensional approach to the suicidal individual, attending to diverse areas of treatment such as interpersonal skills, emotional regulation skills, and the cultivation of balance between an attitude of acceptance and efforts toward change.

PART I

What You Need to Know about Suicide (and about Yourself)

1

Suicide Is an Ugly Word

Job 1: Getting Rid of the Stigma

Soon after deciding to write this book, we discovered that it was going to be easier said than done. A book to help people in distress certainly seemed like a fine idea; but would anyone actually buy a self-help book about *suicide*? And would anyone actually read it? After all, *suicide* is an ugly word!

No one seems to mind buying a book about how to have a healthy heart, read faster, or develop a winning personality, but in most cultures suicide carries a stigma not seen with most other human problems. Take a look at your newspaper's obituary section. It is known that 1.4 percent of all deaths are self-inflicted—more than the number of deaths caused by liver disease, kidney disease, or even homicide. But if your newspaper is like most, its policy is not to report suicide as a cause of death.

While this may be motivated by a well-meaning wish to protect the feelings of surviving family members, why is a death by suicide cause for shame or embarrassment any more than some other cause of death? Answers to this question have many roots (often religious) and go back hundreds of years. As early as the fifth century, St. Augustine denounced suicide as self-murder and a certain road to eternal damnation. By the Middle Ages, legal sanctions had come into play in England, where committing suicide meant that the family lost all claims to the deceased's possessions. As recently as the early 1800s, the French hung the body of a suicide victim from a gallows, and the English pounded a stake through the heart and buried the body at a crossroads. Fortunately, these horrific examples of "blaming the victim" are things of the past. Unfortunately, the stigma of suicide is far from gone. Witness the fact that five states still include suicide in their criminal codes (although these laws are rarely applied).

You may ask, "Well, *shouldn't* suicide and suicidal behavior be stigmatized? Isn't it sinful, after all? Besides, we surely want to do everything we can to discourage self-destructive behavior."

True, we want to do all we can to prevent suicide and suicidal behaviors, but it is unlikely that laying guilt trips on depressed people will be helpful. Aren't depressed people already some of the guiltiest-feeling people around? If guilt were an effective strategy, we would expect depressed people rarely, if ever, to commit suicide. Most depressed people already feel bad about themselves. A threat of moral condemnation is unlikely to have any positive impact on someone who already believes he or she is bad.

Most religions now view suicide as a symptom of an illness rather than a deliberately sinful act. Therefore, they no longer consider it appropriate to condemn a person for an act that was chosen under a cloud of emotional upset and impaired judgment. Moreover, you may be surprised to know that suicide is not specifically prohibited in the Bible (although murder is clearly forbidden, we cannot assume that suicide is a form of murder). If suicide were such a grave transgression, we would expect to see large sections specifically devoted to it.

So, how shall we view suicide? Here's what we recommend:

1. *Get rid of the stigma.* Nothing interferes with therapeutic progress quite like shame. This isn't surprising. If a tennis player believes that it's shameful to need lessons, he'll have a tough time improving his game. Women who are ashamed to see a gynecologist and men who are ashamed to get a prostate exam place themselves at greater risk for undetected cancer. And if you're ashamed of your suicidal thoughts and behaviors, then you aren't very likely to address them through self-help or therapy. Because of this, you could risk losing the opportunity, literally, to save your own life.

Practice thinking of the term *suicidal* in a nonjudgmental way, just as you might think of your friend as being a procrastinator or a couch potato. These are human imperfections that carry with them distinct disadvantages, but they certainly are no cause for condemnation. And these problems all are definitely solvable. This brings us to our second suggestion.

2. *Adopt a problem-solving point of view.* Convince yourself that suicidality* is no more nor less than an attempt (however disadvantageous) to solve a problem—a desperate attempt, when no other viable options are apparent. (Think about it: It makes no sense to believe that an otherwise sane, intelligent person would contemplate self-harm when effective, less painful approaches to problems were apparent.) Whether the predicament is physical

---

* *Suicidality* is a term commonly used to refer to the state of "being suicidal" or to a person's risk of becoming suicidal. *Suicidal* describes a person with any combination of thoughts, feelings, and behaviors that involve the potential for self-inflicted death. A person is considered "suicidal" when he or she is thinking about, talking about, or carrying out deliberate self-harm or self-destruction. These concepts are discussed in more detail in Chapter 2.

pain or the emotional pain of loneliness and loss, painful problems cry out for relief. Is a person to be condemned simply because he or she is having trouble finding a less desperate solution than self-harm?

Also, consider that, unlike shame, the problem-solving view points directly to a solution: The solution to maladaptive problem solving is, quite simply, improved problem solving. At this point, you might be thinking, "Easy for you to say. My problems don't have solutions. If they did, I wouldn't be suicidal!" This leads us to a third suggestion.

3. *Keep an open mind.* Perhaps its not that your problems have no solutions, but just that the solutions are not apparent to you. This is not to suggest that you are missing easy, obvious solutions. If the solutions were easy, you'd have discovered them long ago. Consider the possibility that even intelligent, responsible people occasionally benefit from outside input. Successful businesspeople, major corporations, governmental agencies, and star athletes all use consultants to great advantage. Far from being ashamed, you have every reason to take pride in your openness and willingness to grow by listening and learning.

Real People

The following are two examples of people who, for an assortment of reasons, experienced suicidal thoughts and behaviors. We have changed the names and some of the details to protect their privacy, but the passages below describe real people whom we have seen in our clinical practices. Use these accounts to begin practicing a problem-solving view of suicidality. In other words, practice seeing these individuals as good, decent human beings who, not unlike yourself, had trouble finding more effective, reasonable solutions to their pain than self-harm.

> "Becky" came to our emergency room by ambulance. She had called 911 after swallowing 25 capsules of antidepressant medication. A 17-year-old high-school dropout and mother of an 18-month-old son, she insisted that she hadn't wanted to die, but merely wanted her recently remarried mother to "pay attention to me."
>
> Our work with her on the inpatient unit later revealed that the reasons behind her suicide attempt weren't nearly so simple (they rarely are). Becky had been struggling with feelings of abandonment ever since her father left the family when she was 8 years old. So desperate was she for acceptance that, beginning at age 14, she had remained in a relationship with a boyfriend who called her "stupid" and repeatedly told her that no one else would have her. Behaving much like Becky's father, this boyfriend abandoned her when their baby was born. When Becky's mother, the only reliable person in her life, remarried,

Becky simply did not know how to get her relationship needs taken care of, other than through a desperate act of life endangerment.

"Randy" was a 25-year-old man who came to see me (TE) because he "needed help." During our interview, his eyes remained downcast, his voice almost inaudible. He explained that he had felt depressed "for years" and had recently decided to end his life. An avid hunter, he had taken one of his hunting rifles into the woods near his home, planning never to return. Always looking for positive aspects in situations, I asked Randy what had caused him to return from the woods, choosing life over death. I was taken aback by his reply. "Because I'm a coward," he said bitterly, making eye contact at last; "I didn't have the guts to pull the trigger." This reply reflected what was to become a major focus of therapy for Randy—his long-standing mental habit of savagely criticizing himself for his actions, good or bad. He had not realized that it was this internal self-abuse, not "life," that was the primary source of his pain and that death was by no means the only way of ending that pain.

Prevalence of Suicide

As you reconsider thoughts and feelings about your suicidality, you might wonder whether you have any company. Suicidal individuals often struggle with feeling alone and lonely, different and defective. When they take part in group therapy, they often express amazement that others have had similar thoughts and feelings.

Suicidality in its various forms is surprisingly common. Consider these facts:

- Suicide is the ninth leading cause of death in the United States, accounting for 14 out of every 1000 deaths (1.4 percent).

- More than 30,000 people kill themselves in the United States every year; this is greater than the annual number of homicides.

- More than half of people who commit suicide have never received mental health services.

- Suicide is the number three killer of young adults, ages 15 to 24, second only to accidents and homicide.

- About 17 percent of people suffer from clinical depression at some time in their lifetimes. If untreated, as many as one-sixth of these individuals eventually kill themselves.

These figures don't include people thinking about suicide, threatening suicide, or engaging in nonfatal suicidal behaviors. Knowledge of nonfatal suicidal events is less complete because they are much less public than suicide fatalities. However, surveys have asked people whether they ever attempted or seriously considered suicide. Results show that up to 16 percent of the population have thought about ending their own lives, and up to 4 percent have made actual attempts.

We do not present these statistics to frighten you or to present gloom and doom, but merely to emphasize this: *Suicidality is not a rare, bizarre phenomenon, and you are not a freak.* Having suicidal thoughts and feelings, while certainly undesirable, is not uncommon. So if you find yourself feeling ashamed and thinking thoughts such as "I'm all alone," "This is too terrible to talk about," or "No one would understand this," think again. Remembering the prevalence of suicidality is one way to give yourself the compassion and understanding you need so you can do something about your suicidal feelings.

"Rational" Suicide

People often ask us about rational suicide. The question usually goes something like this: "Don't you think that some peoples lives are so terribly miserable—either from agonizing, terminal illness, or desperate life circumstances—that suicide truly is the best solution? And aren't we rather presumptuous to suggest that someone else should go on living, when we haven't taken a walk in their shoes?"

The question of rational suicide is a legitimate one. Our world is changing rapidly and becoming more complex. One example of change is that people are living longer now than ever before. While this usually is seen as a blessing, there is a dark side: The older a person grows, the more losses he or she suffers in the form of deaths of friends and loved ones, loss of status in a youth-oriented culture, and loss of function due to declining health.

Our new age presents other double-edged swords. For example, medical science understands disease processes, such as Alzheimer's disease and AIDS, better than ever before. By the same token, patients with such illnesses are also better informed and are well aware that their medical future is bleak. They know that, in all probability, they can expect a difficult decline and eventual death from their illness.

All around us, we see society trying to respond to these maddeningly complex issues. We see movies like *Whose Life Is It Anyway?*, in which Richard Dreyfuss plays the part of a formerly healthy, vital man paralyzed from the neck down from an auto accident, who pleads with his caretakers to let him die. We witness the growth of a significant "Right to Die" movement, led by groups such as the Hemlock Society, which makes available information on how to end one's life. Medical societies debate "physician-assisted suicide" at meetings and in journals to address cases in which terminally ill patients can be helped to die rather than live a few more days or weeks in severe, intractable pain. At the other extreme, we follow the exploits of Jack

Kevorkian, the retired pathologist carrying on a one-man crusade by granting desperate people's requests that he help them commit suicide.

What are we to make of all of this? After acknowledging that these are genuinely complex issues, let us remember the words of H. L. Mencken, who said, "For every complex problem there is a simple solution . . . which is wrong." Consider some facts that, while well established, are often lost in the din of this controversy:

- Rigorous studies have shown that, whereas some (though not most) people who committed suicide were terminally ill, almost *all* (at least 95 percent) were suffering from a treatable psychiatric disorder. Unfortunately, most of these people did not receive treatment for their disorder.

- Studies also show that suicidal individuals, terminally ill or not, are almost invariably *clinically depressed*. Because depression interferes significantly with rational thinking, the concept of "rational" suicide loses meaning.

- Depression can be treated successfully in the vast majority of cases; and when the depression is treated, suicidal wishes fade away along with other depressive symptoms.

In other words, even though the case for rational suicide can theoretically be made in rare cases, in the overwhelming majority of cases the problem is not the illness or life circumstances, but the depressive disorder itself. *As long as you are depressed or otherwise emotionally distressed, it is virtually certain that your suicidal thoughts stem from distorted, unrealistically negative thinking. Until and unless this is remedied, "rational" suicide is a virtual impossibility.*

The decision to die is too important to be made by any one person, especially one in the grips of dire circumstances. In cases when suicide (or euthanasia) *might* be an appropriate option, the decision must be made in close consultation with the individual's family and care providers. A team of responsible health care professionals must be involved to assess for depression and ensure that any psychiatric disorder receives appropriate attention. When depression is found and treated, the vast majority of patients feel better and express relief that they did not act on what seemed, at the time, to be rational suicidal ideas.

2

Are You a "Suicidal Person"?

Do you find yourself wondering whether the word *suicidal* really applies to you or your loved one? Perhaps you wonder whether you even need to be reading this book. If you feel at all confused, you're not alone—in fact, you're in pretty good company. Even world-renowned experts have trouble agreeing on what is meant by the terms *suicide* and *suicidal*.

Although some of our patients are very clear about their suicidality, others show considerable confusion. Some say (or worry) that they are suicidal when actually they are not, while some people who are clearly suicidal deny it. It is not necessary to get into the technicalities of suicidology to do your own assessment (although it is essential that a mental health professional be consulted anytime suicidality is suspected).

In this chapter, we will discuss many of the signs and symptoms of suicidality and help you to determine for yourself whether suicidality should be a concern for you or your loved one.

Am I Serious about Suicide or Not?
(Answer: Neither and Both)

Part of the confusion in identifying suicidality arises from black-and-white thinking. This is the false belief that you must be either one or the other: smart or stupid, attractive or ugly, good or bad, suicidal or nonsuicidal. The truth of the matter is that human beings almost always either fall between two extremes (such as "moderately good looking" or "fairly smart") or show some mixture (such as "good and bad").

This also applies to people with self-destructive thoughts. Almost without exception, suicidal people either say or show that they have mixed feelings about living or dying. For example, the individual who insists that he only wants to die often shows in various ways that part of him still wants to live. This may be reflected in certain aspects of a suicide attempt—perhaps the attempt was timed, with or without awareness, to coincide with the arrival of someone who would rescue him. The mere act of communicating suicidal thoughts to someone else suggests that some part of this person wants help so that he can go on living.

The reverse is usually true for the individual who insists that he or she has no desire to die, despite having engaged in dangerous self-harming behavior. We have seen such individuals—from those who have engaged in behaviors as "harmless" as threatening suicide or writing suicide notes to those who have seriously injured themselves or taken potentially lethal overdoses and were rescued only by accident—insist in earnest that they were definitely not suicidal and would never engage in such behavior again.

These individuals typically are not being dishonest. They sincerely believe what they are saying. They simply show by their behavior that they have *ambivalence*—the human capacity to feel two apparently contradictory feelings at the same time. For example, we may simultaneously feel happy for a close friend who has taken a job in a distant city, but also sad or angry that she is leaving. In a similar way, suicidal people almost always have a mixture of a wish to die and a wish to go on living. We have seen people near death from a suicide attempt still gamely cooperating with helpers; and we have seen people who claim to have a great desire to live resist mightily when we ask them to flush their stockpiled pills or remove a gun from the house.

Exercise 1: Exploring Your Two Sides

Use the following form to explore your own ambivalence. In a column labeled "The Hopeful Side," begin listing all of the arguments *against* committing suicide (such as "My family needs me," "It's against my religious beliefs," or "Brighter days might lie ahead"). In the column labeled "The Dark Side," list all of the arguments you can think of *in favor of* committing suicide (in other words, all the reasons why life might not be worth living). There are no right or wrong answers; this portion of the exercise is strictly for getting in touch with where you are.

The second portion of the exercise will help you further expand your awareness. If The Dark Side is the longer or more compelling of your two lists, go back and work on The Hopeful Side. Search for your ambivalence. Think of better times; imagine you're an outside observer, looking at your life objectively. Do whatever you have to do, but add to that list! The goal here is to begin connecting with the life-affirming part of you that you may have lost touch with and that will set the stage for healing in later portions of the book.

If The Hopeful Side is your longer list, we suggest that you first congratulate yourself, but then search for your ambivalence as well. Although

Exercise 1: Exploring Your Two Sides

The Hopeful Side	The Dark Side
1.	1.
2.	2.
3.	3.
4.	4.
5.	5.
6.	6.
7.	7.
8.	8.
9.	9.

having a long life-affirming list puts you a step ahead, we assume that you're reading this book for a reason. So take yourself in your imagination to past (or predicted future) dark periods and write any reasons you find there why life may not be worth living after all. We are not asking you to make things up—only to get in touch with what's already there (or may be there in the future). The purpose here is not to change anything yet, but to dig for what's there as a way of mapping out what you will need to focus on.

Knowing about ambivalence can help you in many ways. Knowing that a subtle but significant wish to die is lurking behind your current posi- tive outlook can help you to make that outlook more solid (for example, if you were to find that part of you believes that being dead would solve all of your problems, this exercise would give you the opportunity to remind yourself that being dead prevents you from enjoying your problem-free state). On the other hand, recognizing a persistent glimmer of a stubborn wish to live, even in the face of severe suicidal thinking, can give you a place to start rebuilding your passion for life.

Two Types of Suicidal People

Perhaps this explanation of ambivalence has helped clarify suicidal states, but one additional source of confusion remains. You may have found your- self thinking, "Sure, my (or my loved one's) therapist asked me to read this book, but I know what a suicidal person is like and I don't (or my loved one doesn't) fit that mold."

This brings us to another vital piece of information about suicidality: Suicidal people come in many different forms. If you think that all suicidal people are crazy, or smart or stupid, or old or young, or divorced, or alco- holic, or any combination of these, then think again. In fact, it's not even true that all suicidal people are depressed.

Although researchers and therapists sometimes talk about suicidality as if all suicidal persons are alike, experienced clinicians know better. Just as the term *cancer* can mean totally different things for different patients, so too does suicidality vary greatly from one individual to another. Unfortunately, modern science has not yet brought us to a place where we can say, "You are a Type XYZ suicidal person, and here's the treatment program for you." However, we can say from clinical experience that suicidal people seem to fall generally into two categories.

The first category is the Depressed/Hopeless type—the group most often referred to in literature about suicide and probably most often thought of when one hears the word *suicide*. This group is exemplified by Randy, the young man described in the previous chapter. He had suffered from depres- sion for many years and reached the point where he was unable to derive pleasure from life. He suffered from sleep problems and loss of appetite and lost interest in things that were important to him. Even more important, he became hopeless—he was convinced that his misery was permanent and that nothing he nor anyone else could do would change this. His thoughts of suicide were motivated by a wish to end his suffering in the only way he thought was left: self-annihilation.

The other category, the Communication/Control type, looks similar on the surface to the Depressed/Hopeless type, but is quite different when we look beneath the surface. True, people in this group express wishes to die and sometimes act on these wishes by harming themselves, but several characteristics set them apart. "Jennifer," for example, was brought to an emergency room by her mother and stepfather. In the midst of a loud argument about her choice of friends, she had swallowed several different medications that she found in the medicine cabinet. At age 16, she had endured many years of family conflict and had in fact been physically abused by her biological father prior to her parents' divorce two years earlier. Things seemed better after her mother remarried, but they deteriorated after her mother gave birth to another child one year later. In a therapy session following her suicide attempt, Jennifer said that she had not wanted to die, but that she had tried everything else to make things better at home and failed, and taking the pills was the only way she knew to communicate her desperation.

Table 2-1 lists other ways that these two groups of suicidal individuals differ. If you wish, you can use it as a checklist to assess which set of characteristics seems to fit you or your loved one better. Some items from both lists might ring true to you, but you probably will find that one list seems more characteristic than the other. Remember that neither of these groups is better or worse, or more or less deserving of care and concern than the other. Research shows that both groups are at a significantly elevated risk for eventually killing themselves. The reason for making the distinction is to help you see how you fit into the big picture we refer to as "suicidal." It also can help therapists and clients in planning what therapy strategy might be most beneficial for a specific individual.

You're Probably Not Suicidal If . . .

In case it's beginning to seem as if everyone on the planet is suicidal, let's consider some groups of people who may worry about being suicidal (or whose loved ones worry they may be), but who probably are not. One such group is persons with **panic disorder**. This is an anxiety disorder characterized by sudden, unpredictable bursts of severe anxiety that produce physical arousal (pounding heart, breathlessness, etc.) and extreme fear of dying or going crazy. In addition to their other concerns, these patients worry that they might go out of control and kill themselves. This fear is sometimes fueled by occasional passing thoughts that they would rather be dead than suffer through another panic attack. Some research evidence does suggest that people with panic disorder attempt suicide at a higher rate than the general population, but this is still a controversial issue.

Several points are worth noting here. First, although people with panic disorder fear that they will lose control, they almost always report that this has never actually happened, even after dozens of high-intensity panic attacks. Moreover, when asked, these patients say that, far from wanting to be dead, they are fearful that they *might* kill themselves. Also, studies about these people when examined closely, reveal that the researchers did not take into account some reasons other than the panic disorder for the patients' greater tendency toward nonfatal suicide attempts. Judging from later published reports showing that people with panic disorder had a suicide rate no greater than the general population, it appears that suicidal behavior is driven by something other than panic disorder.

A caveat: One line of research that has implicated panic disorder as a risk factor for suicide looks at the relatively common combination of panic disorder and depression. As bad as depression is, it doesn't take much imagination to realize how much more miserable a person would be if suffering from both depression and panic attacks (or any other form of severe anxiety). If this describes you, we encourage you to seek help immediately.

Table 2-1: Two Types of Suicidal People	
Depressed/Hopeless	**Communication/Control**
Typical individual is male and middle aged or elderly	Typical individual is female and young
Suicidal episodes often triggered by loss	Suicidal episodes often triggered by conflict
Primary emotional state is despair	Primary emotional state is desperation
Main motivation behind suicidal behavior is to end life	Main motivation behind suicidal behavior is to communicate pain, in hopes of making life better
Attempts are typically secretive and planned well in advance	Attempts are often communicated and may be highly impulsive
Attempts tend to be violent and highly lethal (often guns or hanging)	Attempts tend to be less lethal (usually drug overdoses or cutting)
Typically regrets surviving a suicide attempt	Typically relieved to have survived a suicide attempt
Main focus of therapy is restoration of hope and reduction of negative thinking errors	Main focus of therapy is reduction of conflict and enhancement of problem solving

Anxiety, as well as depression, responds very well to therapy, medication, or a combination of the two.

Another group of people who are sometimes unnecessarily concerned about suicide is people with **obsessive-compulsive disorder (OCD)**. People with this anxiety disorder feel compelled to perform certain nonsensical behaviors (such as washing their hands dozens of times a day or repeatedly checking to make sure the oven is turned off); or they think certain thoughts (such as extreme worry that they might hurt their child, though they have no history of violence). If you have OCD and are not depressed, your worries about committing suicide may merely be a manifestation of your anxiety disorder and not true suicidality. This will likely be a difficult determination for you to make alone, and we recommend a consultation with a mental health professional to sort it out. This anxiety disorder, too, is highly treatable.

We are often asked about people with **unhealthy lifestyles**. Certainly, we all wonder what is going through the minds of loved ones who continue to smoke cigarettes after a heart attack, kids who ride motorcycles recklessly and without helmets, and alcoholics who drive drunk. Indeed, some suicide theorists have proposed *subintentioned* suicide to explain such self-destructive behaviors in people who may not be depressed and who deny that they wish to die.

The problem with this line of reasoning, and the reason we reject it, is that following it to its logical extreme makes the entire concept of suicide practically meaningless; for if a person who smokes cigarettes is suicidal, what about the person who eats too many fatty foods? Those who don't get enough exercise? People who live in cities with air pollution and high crime rates? As you can see, before long we end up believing that practically everyone in the population, in one way or another, is suicidal.

Some people make unwise and unhealthy choices in the way they live their lives; and while therapy might be helpful to them, suicidality is probably not the most useful explanation for their behavior. We maintain that a person is suicidal only if he or she expresses, through words or behavior, extreme emotional pain and an inclination to relieve that pain through self-inflicted harm or death.

Finally, let us consider the issue of brief, **passing thoughts of suicide**. Some patients we have talked to have expressed great concern about the meaning of occasional thoughts such as, "Maybe I'd be better off dead" or "They'd be sorry if I weren't here." Family members sometimes feel grave concern when they hear mention of death, perhaps by a teenage child or elderly family member.

First, you should know that such thoughts are extremely common: Some studies have indicated that half of the population has had such thoughts at one time or another. What's important is to remember that a thought does not equal an act, whether we are talking about suicide, hostile and violent thoughts about an obnoxious coworker, or sexual feelings toward a married neighbor. Suicidal thoughts become important only when they persist, contemplation sets in, or other suicide warning signs are present. If this is the case, immediate action is warranted; if not, concern is probably not necessary. *As always, whenever there is doubt, play it safe by consulting a mental health professional.* Consult the section later in this chapter on "Suicide Risk Factors" for more guidelines on distinguishing passing thoughts from more serious suicidal intent.

Ways You Might Be Fooling Yourself

There are times when people fool themselves—or try to fool others—into thinking that their experience regarding suicide is something other than what it actually is. We human beings do this all the time, in a myriad of different situations: Smokers convince themselves that only other smokers get cancer, criminals convince themselves that they won't get caught, and physically unfit people convince themselves that they really will start exercising . . . tomorrow.

Suicidal people (some, not all) fool themselves in a variety of ways. Here are some that we have encountered through the years, listed in the form of what patients say and our interpretation of what they often really mean.

"I wasn't really serious. (Can I go home now?)" We often hear this from hospital patients who recently made a suicide attempt or serious suicidal threats.

Translation: "I really did want to end my life, but I'm too ashamed to talk about it. To save face, I'll insist that I wasn't really serious. Maybe my problems will go away on their own."

"Yes, I was serious, but now I see the light. (Can I go home now?)" This sounds sincere, but often comes from someone who has not had sufficient time in therapy to truly understand and change the processes behind his or her suicidality.

Translation: "I know I need to get to the bottom of my suicidality and make some changes, but it's too difficult, scary, and time consuming. So I'll just have to take my chances."

"You're taking me much too seriously—everyone thinks about suicide at some time or another. Lighten up!" We sometimes hear this from patients who let down their defenses momentarily, disclosed the extent of their pain and desperation, got frightened, and are now trying to "cover their tracks."

Translation: "It's much too scary for me or my loved ones to deal with the notion of suicide, so I'll minimize its seriousness and continue to carry the burden alone."

"Of course I wanted to die—and I resent your suggesting there was any other reason for my suicidal behavior!" The source of this statement often is the individual who has threatened suicide or made an impulsive, nonmedically dangerous attempt that seemed intended to have an effect on others. The motivation might be to gain attention, but might also be to express anger, elicit sympathy, or cry out for help.

Translation: "I'm afraid that if I look at motives behind my suicidality other than the wish to die, you'll think I'm a manipulator and won't take me seriously. If I miss out on this opportunity to get at what's really behind my self-destructive behavior, then that's just the price I'll have to pay."

"If I were really serious about suicide, I'd have done it by now. If I'm talking about it, I must only want attention." Unfortunately, this dangerous belief is sometimes reinforced by family members and even care providers. The fact is that most people who commit suicide do talk about it beforehand. And while it is true that suicidal thoughts are not uncommon, it is also true that if you have talked about suicide enough to cause concern in others, this is probably sufficient cause to take a close look at it.

Translation: "I, too, am worried about my suicide talk. But it worries me even more that there may actually be something to it, so I'd rather not talk about it."

"Honest—I only wanted attention. Now that the problem is solved, there's no need to talk about it." The first part of this statement is sometimes true—people do sometimes use suicidal threats and behaviors to gain attention, sympathy, or have some other influence on others. But if they then contend that they do not have a problem with suicidality, they fail to realize that they are at risk for similar, and perhaps more dangerous, behavior when future problems arise.

Translation: "I'm pretty embarrassed that I couldn't find a better way to get my needs met, so let's put this genie back in the bottle, and I'll just hope this problem doesn't come up again."

"Just leave me alone; I'm not worth the trouble. I'm just going to end up dead anyway." Statements such as this are usually spoken by people with severe doubts about their lovability and great fear of being abandoned. They sound tough and often reject offers of help from professional helpers, but this is only a cover for their feelings of vulnerability.

Translation: "I'm afraid you'll give up on me, so I'll reject you first. But really, I hope you'll hang in there and help me."

Do you recognize yourself in any of these scenarios? If so, don't give yourself a hard time. If you look back over the translations, you will find consistent themes of shame and fear. It is these feelings that most often prompt us, whether we realize it or not, to fool ourselves or try to fool others. If this is a problem for you, you might return to the previous chapter and review the section on removing the stigma of suicidality.

Remember that suicidal thoughts and behaviors are human problems like any other (anger problems, gambling too much, having a hard time saying "no," etc.) and are nothing to be ashamed of. If someone, whether a family member, friend, or counselor, in any way suggests that your suicidality is something to be ashamed of, he or she is mistaken. In that case, we suggest you find someone else who will make it easier for you to talk about it. Minimizing or otherwise distorting your suicidality can have highly dangerous consequences. Talking about it candidly, even though it doesn't show your best side, is the best shot at a start on a new and healthy path.

Suicide Risk Factors

Although suicidal risk is often clear-cut (for example, you may be fully aware of the seriousness of your wish to die, or your loved one may have made a life-endangering attempt), there also exists a gray area. How can you distinguish between what are simply passing thoughts in a moment of pain or an angry but superficial outburst versus suicidal thoughts and behaviors that are cause for major concern?

Certain risk factors that have been shown to be associated with suicide are summarized in Table 2-2 and are described here.

Psychological disorder. Depression, substance abuse, and schizophrenia are the illnesses most often associated with suicide risk, but any psychological disorder raises suicide risk to some extent. Niney-five percent of people who kill themselves suffer from some psychological disorder. Both depression and schizophrenia have eventual suicide rates as high as 15 percent.

History of suicide attempts. One of the best-known principles in behavioral science is that future behavior tends to be consistent with past behavior. In the area of suicide, studies have shown that the best predictor of death by suicide is a history of previous suicide attempts.

Hopelessness. Research has demonstrated that hopelessness is a critical connecting link between depression and suicide. If you or your loved one experiences difficulty imagining when and how things will get better, this is a sure sign that professional help is needed.

Family history of suicide. Studies have shown that suicide often runs in families. Whether this is due to a genetically transmitted biological vulnerability, behavioral modeling effects, or some combination of factors is not known, but thoughts or talk of suicide in a person with a family history of suicide should be taken very seriously.

A specific plan. If suicidal thinking has proceeded from vague abstraction to a specific plan, immediate attention is required. The more specific the plan, the greater the risk. Someone who has considered a method of committing suicide, and even thought of a time and a place to do it, is at much greater risk than someone who has not considered a specific plan.

Making preparations. When suicidal thinking proceeds from a plan to actual preparations, suicide risk increases significantly. Preparations may take the form of composing a suicide note, putting things in order (such as writing a will or taking out life insurance), storing up pills, obtaining a weapon, or mending fences with relatives. Suicidal teenagers sometimes give away prized possessions as a way of preparing for death.

Severe symptoms of depression and anxiety. These include hopelessness, agitation, sleep problems, loss of appetite, chronic anxiety and worry, panic attacks, loss of interest, abuse of alcohol or other substances, and severe self-criticism. These symptoms almost always respond well to psychological or pharmacological intervention. However, when left unchecked, sufferers sometimes conclude that they can no longer stand the burden life has placed on them.

Isolation and withdrawal. Hopelessness and despair tend to grow stronger in the absence of support from caring others. Isolation and withdrawal increase suicide risk because cutting off ties with other people magnifies feelings of aloneness and precludes many problems from being solved.

Perception of insufficient reasons for living. Dr. Marsha Linehan has shown that suicidal people have considerable trouble listing reasons for staying alive. This is probably not because the reasons weren't there, but

---

Table 2-2: Suicide Risk Factors

Psychological disorder

History of suicide attempts

Hopelessness

Family history of suicide

A specific plan

Making preparations

Severe symptoms of depression and anxiety

Isolation and withdrawal

Perception of insufficient reasons for living

Presence of a firearm in the home

because emotional distress had made it difficult for them to see or remember those reasons. People in comparison groups, on the other hand, waxed eloquent, listing everything from family ties, career goals, and spiritual beliefs to ice cream and flowers in the spring. Lack of *perceived* reasons for living is exactly what common sense tells us it is, a symptom of depression and a sign of suicide risk.

Presence of a firearm in the home. Dr. David Brendt and his colleagues at the University of Pittsburgh showed in a study of suicide attempts that a potent predictor of which teenagers died from their suicide attempt was the presence of a firearm in the home. In addition to viewing this as a risk factor, *you must remove all firearms from your home if any family member shows signs of suicidality.* This is not optional! Safe firearm practices, such as locking guns away, have not been shown to be helpful; however, solid research does show that lack of availability in the community effectively reduces the suicide toll.

If you or a loved one are free from these risk factors, then passing thoughts of suicide are probably no cause for alarm. On the other hand, you should seek help immediately if you or a loved one is experiencing suicidal thoughts in combination with risk factors on this list. Trying to rationalize or explain away suicidal thoughts or impulses in the presence of known suicide risk factors is dangerous and unwise.

Assessment by a Mental Health Professional

Although we have shown in this chapter how you can assess signs and symptoms of suicide risk in yourself or a loved one, a valid suicide assessment, like any examination with life-and-death implications, should be done by a professional trained in what to look for and what interventions to pursue. Although most mental health professionals (psychologists, psychiatrists, social workers, and counselors) are competent to conduct a suicide risk assessment, we must tell you that, as among doctors, lawyers, stockbrokers, and other professionals, competence levels vary. Often, nonpsychiatric physicians, ministers, and lay counselors are unprepared to explore for suicidality or to ask the detailed questions necessary for a thorough assessment.

Therefore, we encourage you to exercise intelligent self-interest. If you visit a counselor, doctor, clergyperson, or any other helper to talk about your problems, and he or she fails to inquire about suicide, *bring it up yourself.* There is no law that says you must wait to be asked or cannot volunteer information. If you feel that suicidality is brushed over too lightly, seek out someone who gives the matter its due. Remember, your life or that of your loved one might be at stake.

3

"What's *Wrong* with You?"
(What Makes People Suicidal)

The title of this chapter is intended not only to convey the chapter's content but also to reflect the experience of many suicidal individuals. How many readers, we wonder, have heard such questions from impatient friends and family members: "Whats *with* you?" "Why don't you just snap out of it?" "Why can't you just be like everybody else?" Indeed, how many suicidal persons have heard these questions in accusatory tones from *themselves* while looking into the mirror?

When asked in critical tones, these questions are of little use and serve only to make you feel bad. On the other hand, it is perfectly reasonable for you, as a suicidal person or a suicidal person's friend or family member, to ask sincerely what it is about people with suicidal tendencies that sets them apart from nonsuicidal people and places them at higher risk for self-inflicted death. So let us plunge into the question of why some people become suicidal.

The instinct to survive is something that all of us possess to some degree and, indeed, seems to be innate to all living creatures. When someone wishes to die, it seems in direct opposition to one of the fundamental aspects of our existence—so we generally assume that something must be wrong with anyone who has suicidal feelings. However, we can go much further than such labels in understanding why people sometimes become suicidal.

As you read this, remember that whatever it is that has gone "wrong" does not make you a bad person or mean that you can't be helped. We expect that you will recognize aspects of yourself or your loved one. Recognizing these characteristics is an important first step in coming to grips with, and ultimately solving, the problems that produce suicidal thoughts and feelings. We begin by looking at common psychological disorders, and then turn to other factors, such as certain thinking patterns and stressful life events, that fan the flames of suicidal crises.

Psychological Disorders

Rigorous studies have shown that 95 percent of people who commit suicide were suffering from a treatable psychological disorder. Much the same can be said for people who make nonfatal suicide attempts. Sadly, even in this day of high technology and "miracle cures," the majority of people who could benefit from mental health treatment never receive it. This makes suicidal deaths all the more tragic and often leaves bereaved friends and relatives asking themselves the painful question, "Why didn't I insist that he (or she) get help?" Take a close look at the following disorders, and see if any of them seem familiar. We start with a discussion of the "big three" categories of psychological disorders that contribute to suicide risk: depression, substance abuse, and psychotic disorders.

Depression

If you are clinically depressed, you suffer from something much more than a simple case of the blues. Depression is a major, life-threatening illness that warrants priority attention. If this sounds to you like a couple of soft-hearted psychologists trying to be nice to people who only need a kick in the pants, consider this fact: *Left untreated, one depressed person in six will commit suicide.* That's a mortality rate of about 15 percent. Any illness with fatality figures this high would be considered a major illness; yet our society (including many insurance companies and health plans), still mired in the stigma of the past, continues to treat depression as a low-priority concern.

Clinical depression, as well as the depressive phase of manic-depressive disorder, involves an entire set of severe symptoms that last for at least two weeks (usually much longer), day in and day out. You may find that you are unable to enjoy the things you used to enjoy, including many of your favorite activities and your interactions with other people. You probably feel down on yourself, too—diminished confidence, increased guilt, shame, and unworthiness. Your energy level is probably low, making it difficult to carry out even day-to-day tasks of living, much less handle major changes, projects, or problems. Your concentration is probably disrupted by negative, ruminative thoughts about how badly things are going and how badly you are doing. Your expectations for the future seem bleak, so you feel trapped in a state of misery. To top it all off, your sleep patterns may be disrupted, and you have either lost your appetite or you find yourself over-eating to soothe the emotional pain. Your interest in sex may be greatly reduced, along with your general interest in life itself.

Being clinically depressed does not necessarily mean being suicidal. However, when depression becomes complicated by other psychological disorders or life stressors (such as those described later in the chapter) odds that you will have thoughts about suicide increase.

Although we know for a fact that periods of clinical depression sometimes go away by themselves after a few months, it is risky to do nothing about your depression, because depressed people often cannot see that things will get better, and this alone can make them more apt to consider suicide. Further, the symptoms of depression often have a self-perpetuating quality that can lead to worsening of the condition if nothing is done to treat it.

For example, if you suffer from low levels of energy and motivation, you probably will become less active and engage in fewer of the activities that you typically would enjoy. This puts you in double jeopardy. First, inactivity can worsen depression because it is associated with a depletion of an important chemical in the brain called serotonin. As the serotonin level decreases, mood usually deteriorates as well, which further depletes your energy. Thus, a vicious cycle begins. Second, if you are doing fewer and fewer things that you would typically enjoy, you will experience less and less pleasure, and your sense of confidence and accomplishment will suffer as well.

Clinical depression also is reflected in how you think. Dr. Aaron Beck (1967) has written extensively about the "cognitive triad," which entails a person's thoughts about (1) the self, (2) life itself, including the events and the people around you, and (3) the future. Depressed people tend to have negatively biased thinking patterns. As a result, you may be down on yourself, you may lose interest in others or view life in a generally negative way, and you will probably hold out little hope that things will ever improve in your life. You may be at risk for engaging in self-defeating behaviors, such as drifting away from the people who care about you, quitting important activities, avoiding new opportunities, and neglecting your health. This process can become so extreme that death may begin to look like the only viable option.

You must remember that *clinical depression is highly treatable:* 80 percent or more of individuals who seek treatment get significantly better. If you suffer from depression, you may feel hopeless and suicidal; but be aware that suicidal thoughts dangerously overlook the fact that you will almost certainly get well over time, especially with the proper treatment. It is crucial that you remember that hopelessness is a *symptom* of your disorder and not an accurate appraisal of your situation. Hopelessness will disappear with treatment, along with the other depressive symptoms. If you still don't believe that you can get well, because you feel as if you have been depressed all your life, please refer to the section on personality patterns a little later on in the chapter.

Alcohol and Drug Abuse

Whenever we introduce a mood-altering chemical into our bodies, our perceptions become distorted. Sometimes this can be a pleasant experience, such as taking a minor tranquilizer to help with the anxiety of flying in an airplane or relaxing with a glass of wine with dinner. However, it is this very effect that motivates some people to use alcohol and other drugs as a primary way to soothe emotional upset.

Unfortunately, when people come to rely routinely on mood-altering substances in order to feel good or to cope, they set themselves up for considerable trouble. This is true for a number of reasons:

1. Regular overuse of a psychoactive chemical (including beer and wine) sooner or later leads to biochemical tolerance and addiction.

2. Use of psychoactive substances distorts thinking and feelings, and the more substance used, the more distortion.

3. Physical health begins to decline over time.

4. Alcohol and many other drugs have a depressant effect on the brain, even if the initial experience is a "high." Therefore, a depressed person who uses substances in order to self-medicate unwittingly makes himself or herself even more depressed.

5. Alcohol and drugs cause a suppression of the body's natural painkillers. When the effects of the alcohol and drugs wear off, the user is in more pain than when he or she started. This often leads the person to use more drugs and alcohol, and a vicious cycle is started.

6. Alcohol and drugs cause loss of inhibitions, often impairing judgment and other thought processes. Intoxicated persons are likely to do things that they would not ordinarily do. This includes dangerous behaviors such as driving while intoxicated, engaging in unsafe sex, and impulsively attempting suicide. As many as half of suicides involve the use of drugs and alcohol in the hours leading up to the time of death.

7. When a person habitually uses alcohol and drugs to deal with problems and upset feelings, the problems remain unsolved and frequently get worse. Further, the individual fails to learn valuable problem-solving skills and gain confidence in dealing with adverse life circumstances. What often follows is a lowering of self-esteem and an increase in the perceived need to use substances in order to find an escape.

8. The notion of using alcohol and drugs in order to self-medicate a depression or anxiety reflects a common misconception. In fact, far from medicating the disorder, drugs and alcohol make the individ-

ual less able to cope effectively. It is only when people *stop* using substances and learn to solve their problems through more effective means that they start feeling better.

9. Abuse of drugs and alcohol can lead people to become so chemically addicted that they develop another problem (the addiction) that they are unable to beat. This typically leads to a worsened sense of helplessness, hopelessness, and shame that may in turn lead to suicidal impulses.

10. Abusing alcohol and other drugs almost inevitably leads to tangible personal losses that can make depression significantly worse. Such losses include loss of relationships (even marriages), loss of employment and income, loss of possessions, loss of privileges such as driving, loss of reputation and status, and various combinations of these. When such losses accumulate, depression and hopelessness increase and reasons for living decline.

In summary, abuse of alcohol and/or other drugs, while sometimes reducing pain in the short term, actually increases the risk of attempting or committing suicide. This is especially true when depression is in the picture. In fact, many people have what is known in the field as a *dual diagnosis*—both substance dependence and a depressive (or other) disorder. This is a potentially deadly combination that absolutely warrants professional intervention.

Psychotic Disorders

The term *psychosis* refers to a broad range of psychological conditions and a wide range of degrees of severity. Most prominent is schizophrenia, which carries a suicide risk comparable to that of depression. Affective disorders, such as major depression and bipolar affective disorder (manic-depressive illness), sometimes involve psychotic states as well. In essence, a person in the midst of a psychotic episode has significant difficulty distinguishing what is real from what is not. Examples range from the person who steadfastly but erroneously believes that the CIA is after him, to the individual who is convinced that she is personally to blame for the floods in the Midwest, to the fellow who hears voices in his head that command him to kill himself.

Most psychotic conditions carry with them an elevated risk of suicide. Such symptoms require immediate treatment, almost always involving medication and sometimes requiring a protective stay in the hospital. Less blatant psychotic symptoms can contribute to suicide risk as well. Generally referred to as delusions, these are extreme, mistaken beliefs, such as being responsible for all the evil in the world or having something eating at one's insides. Suicide thus becomes a misguided way to "save" the world or avoid the ravages of an imagined illness.

Most psychotic states can be controlled with medication. Recent evidence shows that cognitive therapy can also be effective in treating these problems. Even if you have suffered from psychotic symptoms, you have every reason to expect that your condition will respond to treatment.

Personality Patterns

When we speak of a person's *personality*, we mean patterns of thoughts, emotions, and behaviors that a person exhibits in many different situations and that have appeared in some form or another throughout the person's life. For example, we would probably not label a 3-year-old child an "angry, bitter person" because he threw a temper tantrum. However, if that same youngster was prone to such outbursts, showed few signs of sociability and happiness, and grew up to become someone who was often hostile toward others, we might be more inclined to describe him as having an angry, bitter personality.

One of the hallmarks of good mental health is a certain flexibility in reactions to the thousands of situations that life throws our way. Flexibility makes us more adaptable to life's demands, increases chances that our needs will be met, and lowers the chances that we will suffer from depression and despair.

Everyone feels hurt when they are rejected by someone important to them. However, you would be more inclined to recover from this blow if you were receptive to the kind words and care of someone else and you felt confident that you were basically a lovable person. On the other hand, if you were the kind of person who chronically felt unworthy of love, you might be devastated even by casual slights, and you might not be reassured by others who spoke kindly of you. This sort of extreme, inflexible, adverse reaction suggests a dysfunctional personality pattern.

All of us have quirks in our personalities, and most of these are fairly innocuous. Indeed, they are part of what makes us unique individuals. There are, however, two reliable signs that such quirks may be more serious. One is when a person experiences chronic difficulties in relationships with other people. The other is when a person does not like the kind of person he or she is and feels as if he or she cannot change.

It is true that habits are hard to break, but having the motivation to change can help overcome great obstacles. The old notion that you "can't teach an old dog new tricks" simply has not been supported by research on the outcome of psychotherapy. Some of our clients tell us that they have been depressed all their lives. They maintain that, since they cannot remember having been happy, the sadness must be part of who they are. They worry that getting over their depression and suicidality would require becoming different people. Since they don't believe that this is possible, they may conclude that suicide is the only way to escape from the misery of who they are.

It is perhaps understandable that they would develop this viewpoint, given the years of pain they have experienced. However, personality and identity are neither entirely inborn nor permanently fixed; they are shaped by learning as well. One aim of therapy is to help people improve the quality of their lives by teaching them to make changes in their approaches to life, even if it feels foreign at first. Over time, this can literally change someone's personality.

The downside is that the process does take time. It is often difficult for someone who has been in emotional pain for a long time to be patient and persevere through the hard work of recovery. This is where the support of a good therapist and understanding loved ones can be very helpful. But it is even possible to make significant changes on your own if you remember that hard work will be rewarded with better times ahead.

Thinking Patterns

As psychologist Albert Ellis (1994) has shown for more than four decades, people's problem emotions and behaviors can be broken down into three components, which came to be known as the "A-B-Cs" of Rational-Emotive Therapy. As shown in Table 3-1, these letters stand for the Activating event, the Belief, and the emotional or behavioral Consequences. This is the process by which a merely bad event can turn into an imagined catastrophe with life-endangering implications.

Consider "James," a 27-year-old unemployed former highway department worker, who upon learning that his wife was filing for a divorce, drank two six-packs of beer and locked himself in his room. Because James would not respond to her calls and because she knew that there was a handgun in the nightstand, his wife called the police, who were able to coax James out of the room. When he sobered up, James acknowledged that he was suicidal, commenting that rejection by his wife was yet one more blow in a long string of failures.

As shown in Table 3-1, James thought that his wife's actions proved that he was a total failure. In this respect, it is not difficult to understand why he would begin to view suicide as an appropriate course of action. But is this the only possible interpretation of an impending divorce? Obviously not; otherwise, we would expect everyone who was rejected by a mate to become suicidal. In reality, we see an almost infinite variety of ways that people react to rejection, and we can understand this variety by examining how people think about such an event. Table 3-1 lists a few Bs that differ markedly from James's interpretation of divorce. Notice what a dramatically different outcome results from a different interpretation.

The A-B-C model is the cornerstone of cognitive therapy: The way we think powerfully influences the way we feel and behave. Thus, when we unrealistically magnify our problems and minimize our assets, we set ourselves up for unnecessary emotional distress. Nobody is immune from the

Table 3-1: A-B-C Model of Emotional Distress

Activating Event	Belief	Consequences
Rejection by mate	This proves what a failure I am.	depression, alcohol abuse, suicidal thoughts and actions
	This proves what a bitch my wife is!	rage, verbally or physically abusive behavior
	I'll never be able to cope on my own.	anxiety, desperate attempts to find a new mate
	I'll really miss her. This will hurt for a while, but I'll be okay if I take care of myself.	sadness, positive coping behaviors
	Free at last! I can't wait to hit the dating scene again.	joy, increased socializing

occasional bout of pessimism or overworry, but some people think in a way that makes negative emotions a regular part of life. In fact, negative basic attitudes about yourself, your life, and your future can actually put you at chronic risk of hurting yourself.

Problematic thinking patterns are not seen only in people who have psychological disorders. However, they seem more severe and rigid in people who suffer from clinical depression, manic-depression (bipolar affective disorder), anxiety disorders, personality disorders, substance abuse disorders, and other diagnostic categories. Below are some of the more common thinking errors found in people with suicidal tendencies.

Maladaptive Beliefs about Achievement and Control

Although it is generally healthy to strive for success and a sense of control in your life, it can be hazardous to take this to one or the other extreme. For example, if you believe that you must do things perfectly, and you become upset and self-reproachful whenever you make a mistake, you will rarely be able to relax. To err is human. It is unrealistic and unfair to demand that you should never make a mistake or that you should always be at your best.

Such an attitude will make it difficult for you to like yourself or to enjoy a well-earned sense of accomplishment. In extreme instances, it can lead to suicidality. The college student who overdoses after losing her perfect grade point average or the businessman who shoots himself following a financial reversal are cases in point.

At the other extreme are people who are convinced that they are inadequate and incompetent and therefore either ignore their actual success or don't even try. We hear this in people who say things such as "I can't go back to school, I'm not smart enough" or "I'll just mess things up anyway, so what's the point of trying to improve my life?" Such attitudes reflect a damaging lack of self-confidence. When someone has such a blatant disregard for himself or herself, the act of self-harm may not seem out of the question.

Dysfunctional Attitudes about Love and Relationships

Human beings are social animals. To be healthy and happy, we must see ourselves as worthy of being loved, and we must form emotional bonds with others. If we are lucky, our parents (or other important role models) foster our sense of lovability early in life. If this is learned well, it helps us to overcome the pain of rejection that inevitably occurs over the course of our lives. If we were not fortunate enough to have had parents who nurtured us and made us feel loved, it is still possible to get these needs met later in life by others. However, it is more likely that we will have acquired some troublesome beliefs about relationships.

For example, you may believe that you are not worth anything unless you are married or in a romantic relationship. Or you may become overly dependent on a loved one to provide you with your sense of identity. If this is true, the break up (or feared break up) of your relationship can leave you with a shaky sense of who you are—indeed, you might feel, and mistakenly believe, that you have lost *everything*. Sadly, many people have killed themselves because they felt like nothing without a relationship or because they interpreted a break up as evidence that they would never be loved.

Maladaptive beliefs about your lovability can present difficulties well beyond how you react to relationship problems. Such beliefs can cause you to ignore the fact that others do indeed love you. They can make it difficult for you to believe and accept the positive attention that others may be trying to give you. They can make you feel alone, even when you are surrounded by caring people. They can convince you that you should kill yourself rather than wait around for what you believe to be inevitable mistreatment and abandonment.

Staying in an abusive relationship is another sign of faulty beliefs about your lovability. You may believe that a bad relationship is better than no relationship, that nobody else would have you, and that you wouldn't be able to take care of your own emotional needs if you left. If the situation seems intolerable, you may opt to hurt yourself rather than try to start over on your own. This is drastic action, but you will have a hard time seeing it any other way until you make changes in your beliefs about your love and attachments.

Maladaptive Beliefs about the Future

Hopelessness has been shown to be a crucial connecting link between depression and suicide. Hopelessness is extremely common in people who are prone to self-harming behavior and suicide. No one among us can predict the future with 100-percent accuracy, yet people with self-destructive habits and intentions often feel certain that the future holds only misery for them.

We hear this attitude in people who say things such as "I'm going to be dead by the time I'm thirty anyway, so what do I care if I overdose on drugs or get HIV?" or "I'm not getting any younger and my life is going downhill. I might as well end it all now," or "Nothing I do ever works out. I'll always be unhappy. Nothing will ever change," and similar sentiments.

If you have a bleak view of your future, you are missing an ingredient needed to survive and recover from life's travails: *hope*. Hope is what helps people through bleak times. We see this in the parent who successfully raises children without a partner, in the person who returns to school late in life and earns an advanced degree, in the individual who manages to live for days in the wilderness until rescued, and in the person who defies and defeats her doctor's prediction that she has only a few months to live.

The human spirit can overcome adversity; hope is the fuel that makes the spirit burn brightly. This is not false hope, mind you, but hope that is rooted in taking a stand, having a plan, and actively moving forward in spite of adversity.

Underestimating Reasons for Living

A cognitive distortion common in severely depressed individuals is a tendency to magnify the negative and minimize or disqualify the positive. To add insult to injury, such persons sometimes hear criticism from others (some of whom are well meaning and some of whom are simply exasperated), who say, "You make mountains out of molehills" or "You don't appreciate what you have." Judgmental tone aside, this may be true.

Most suicidal people do in fact minimize or overlook reasons for living. This is not intentional. Rather, it happens because their depression casts a pall over their perceptions, making it truly seem that there is insufficient reason to go on living. Other people often can see more clearly what the person stands to lose if he or she commits suicide.

Reasons for living differ from one person to another, and it would be virtually impossible to enumerate them all. However, it is important to re-

Table 3-2: Commonly Reported Reasons for Living

To see my children grow up.

So I can travel to places I've always wanted to visit.

To see if I can find the relationship I want.

To continue to advance in my work.

So I can retire and relax for the first time in my life.

So I can help others with the same problems I have.

So I can finish my novel.

My wife needs me, and I need her.

There is much I still want to do and to learn.

I am a worthwhile person, and I deserve some happiness.

Life has many simple pleasures to enjoy:

> the smell of coffee in the morning
>
> soaking in a hot tub
>
> a cold beer after mowing the lawn
>
> the sound of children's laughter
>
> the beach
>
> ice cream
>
> Carol Burnett reruns
>
> back rubs
>
> rock 'n' roll (or jazz, classical, country, etc.)

No matter how ugly life can be, beauty still abounds:

> paintings by Michelangelo and Degas
>
> flowers in the spring and leaves in the fall
>
> sunsets
>
> Mozart
>
> Sophia Loren
>
> Sean Connery
>
> a baby's soft skin
>
> a kind word from a stranger

member, as a general principle, that reasons for living can be large or small; and they certainly don't have to be earthshaking accomplishments or aspirations. Table 3-2 shows a sampling of answers we have received when we have asked our clients about their reasons for living.

Exercise 2: Your Reasons for Living

Start an ongoing list of your own reasons for living. Begin with the reasons you have chosen to continue living up to this point in your life. If you wish, you can start with a few of the reasons listed in Table 3-2 that ring true to you. Add at least one reason to your list every day. Remember, your ability to list reasons for living will be influenced considerably by your mood on any given day. Pay attention to how many more reasons you can list on days you feel good compared to days when you are depressed. Does this mean that reasons for living cease to exist on days you are depressed? Definitely not! It merely illustrates in a powerful way how emotional upset can obscure your vision, blocking out positive memories and thoughts. A personal Reasons for Living list can be a vital part of your "emotional first-aid kit" to help you recall reasons you can't think of during periods of depression.

Ineffective Problem Solving _X_   *Key Point*

The ability to recognize a problem, define it clearly, and think through possible solutions is a valuable skill. There is no way to avoid life's problems, so what separates those who are satisfied with their lives from those who are not often has to do with how well the person *solves* those problems.

When problems are overlooked or ignored, they almost always grow. This can lead to your feeling overwhelmed and to the sense that the problems cannot be managed. Ignoring a problem will not make it go away; the adage that "things take care of themselves if you leave them alone" simply isn't true. *People* solve problems, and not by luck, magic, or the simple passage of time. Furthermore, people are more apt to succeed in solving problems if they catch them early, face up to them with hope and confidence, and work out a plan of action.

One of our clients, upon hearing that she might need to work on her problem-solving skills, reacted angrily: "Is that what you think—that my life is actually problem free and that I just don't know how to cope? Well, that's easy for you to say. You don't have to deal with my hyperactive son, busted water pipes, and neighborhood drug dealers. Listen, my problems are real, and I resent your suggesting they're only in my head!"

If you notice yourself having thoughts like these, let us make something very clear: *To suggest that you practice improving your problem-solving skills in no way implies that your problems are not real.* Studies have shown that suicidal individuals actually do have more life stressors to deal with than people who are not suicidal. If you believe that you have more problems than the average human being, it is even more important for you to develop excellent problem-solving skills in order to address them. Chapter 9 will give you some guidance in doing this.

We wish that problem solving were as much a part of the school curriculum as reading, writing, and arithmetic—it's that important. It is a skill that takes time, effort, and practice, but it more than pays for the effort by saving you untold amounts of grief in the long run. Let's look at an example:

> "Steven" prided himself on being a "spur-of-the-moment kind of guy." He stated that he never planned things or thought things through systematically because "you can't count on things working out the way you want them to, anyway." At first glance, this appeared to be a confident fellow who knew who he was and what he wanted; but nothing could have been further from the truth. Steven was addicted to cocaine, faced a court hearing, had destroyed his credit rating, had alienated his girlfriend and his family, and chronically felt suicidal. Therapy focused heavily on helping him change his style so that he was more willing to confront his problems honestly and methodically.

Suicidal people sometimes feel so overwhelmed by their problems that they try to solve them by desperate, unwise means, or they attempt to escape from them altogether. For example the individual who tries to solve a financial problem by borrowing from a loan shark actually creates greater problems for himself in the long run. You or a loved one may have engaged in self-harming behavior as a way to solve a relationship problem, only to find that any benefit from such behavior was only temporary; likewise for the person who seeks solace from daily stressors through drugs and alcohol.

If you feel that your problems have gotten out of hand, that your life is out of control, and that you can no longer cope with your stress, you might begin to view death as the only solution available to you. This is the ultimate example of maladaptive problem solving. *Suicide does not solve problems.* At best, it ends your awareness of the problems; but you don't get to enjoy the benefits. Suicide also creates terrible new problems for those you leave behind. The only problem that never can be solved is death itself. As long as you're alive, you at least have a chance.

Stressful Life Events

Another influence that contributes to suicide risk is stress. Stressful events are part of being alive. We all sometimes experience events that hurt us and test our resolve to carry on. Ideally, these experiences pass as a routine, albeit painful, part of the life cycle and contribute to our maturity. Unfortunately, such events as illness, death of a loved one, or financial setbacks sometimes arrive in clusters, making it difficult to cope. If you already suffer from a disorder such as clinical depression, an added negative event in life might feel overwhelming. Furthermore, if you hold some of the maladaptive beliefs just described, you might be quite vulnerable to stress.

In the next section, we describe some major life stressors that contribute to suicide risk. These events in and of themselves do not make a person suicidal. However, if many of these take place close together in time and coincide with a person's clinical depression and maladaptive beliefs, suicidality can become an issue.

Separation or Loss

The loss of an important relationship, whether through circumstance, conflict, or death, can be a crushing blow, especially if such losses occur repeatedly. If you have experienced significant losses early in life, such as the death of a parent when you were a child, you may be particularly sensitive to the loss of love that occurs when someone you care about in adulthood leaves you or dies. Similarly, if you lack a supporting cast of caring people in your present life, the loss of one special person may make you feel as if you have lost everything. This is especially true if you lack a secure sense of your own worth and identity.

While interpersonal losses may be unavoidable, it does not necessarily follow that you will always be alone. It also does not diminish the meaningfulness of those relationships that you do have. Everything hinges on *what you believe*. Examine the following beliefs to see if any sound familiar to you:

- My life is worth nothing if I am not in a relationship.

- If someone I love stops loving me, I am no longer worthy of being loved by anyone, ever again.

- I can't cope without my loved one. If I am left alone, I won't be able to go on.

- It's all my fault that my loved one is gone. I deserve to die.

- Everybody always ends up leaving me. The only way I can prevent this is if *I* leave everyone by killing myself.

Beliefs like these can transform an incident of separation and loss into a life-and-death situation for you. Holding such beliefs can even make you want to hurt yourself just at the thought that you might lose someone. They are also hard to give up because they feel so "right" and so much a part of who you are. However, we will teach you how to challenge and change them later in this book.

Injury, Illness, and Loss of Freedom

Some people become suicidal partially as a result of debilitating physical illness or injury. Unremitting pain, irreversible limitations, the prospect of progressive decline, and the loss of control over one's own functioning can sometimes lead to a wish to die.

Consider the following scenarios: (1) A person becomes paralyzed as a result of an accident, believes that all chances of having a meaningful life are over, and lapses into a deep depression; (2) a cancer patient becomes fed up with the pain associated with her chemotherapy and radiation treatments and decides to cease all treatment, choosing instead to die quickly; (3) a man who is HIV-positive decides to kill himself with an overdose of sleeping pills at the first sign of an AIDS-related set of symptoms; (4) an older man whose memory starts to fail believes that he has Alzheimer's disease and decides to shoot himself "to spare my family" and (5) a woman who has suffered disfiguring burns becomes suicidal as a result of the chronic pain, the prospect of numerous surgeries, and rejection of her own appearance.

We can all sympathize deeply with each of these people's predicaments. If we put ourselves in their positions, we might even conclude that suicide seems "understandable." Nonetheless, it would be premature and hazardous to state definitively that suicide is the only choice in these cases. To do so would be to ignore true reasons for hope and to risk that we might be tragically incorrect in our assumptions that the conditions are hopeless.

For example, many people lead full, productive, and meaningful lives following paralyzing injuries. Similarly, we know of people with supposedly terminal illnesses who had unexplainable recoveries. Many people have reported that their illnesses have made them appreciate life even more and have inspired them to become closer to the important people in their lives. Studies have shown that the main difference between terminally ill patients who become suicidal and those who don't is the presence of clinical depression in the patients who are suicidal. In other words, the culprit is not the illness or injury, but depression.

Self-diagnosis is a bad idea. Suppose the man who thought he had Alzheimer's disease was wrong. By choosing to kill himself rather than suffer a decline, he could be robbing himself and his loved ones of many years of healthy functioning. The man who wants to die because he dreads experiencing AIDS-related illnesses actually could be years away from serious complications. By choosing to kill himself, he guarantees that he will not live long enough to benefit from medical advances in years to come. The woman with the debilitating burns may not be able to bear the thought of so many painful surgeries, yet it may be just these operations that will give her a chance to regain a life that she will enjoy and value. The theme here is one which we will repeat: *It is not the event itself which causes the suicidality.* It is the loss of hope, together with the sense that you cannot handle the suffering, that fuels the thoughts of suicide.

Loss of Status

We are aware of some instances when a person has committed suicide after a major change in lifestyle, a humiliating experience, or a similar "fall from grace." Examples include an actor who killed himself when his career stalled, a politician who shot himself at a press conference rather than go to prison, and a student who committed suicide after learning she had not been accepted into medical school.

Such reactions are difficult for some to understand, since these losses seem trivial compared to losing a loved one or suffering from a horrible medical condition. To understand, we must consider how such losses are interpreted. If the individual believes that failure is a fate worse than death and that almost any lack of success makes her or him an abject failure, then suicidality following a reversal of fortune becomes more understandable.

Here are examples of thoughts that might fuel such an outlook:

- Now that I am no longer wealthy (powerful, well known, prestigious), I will lose all my friends and I will be all alone.

- Life is not worth living if I can't be the best.

- I will never be able to make a comeback.

- Now that I've failed, no one will ever respect me again.

These are shaky assumptions on which to base a life-and-death decision. They are based on an exaggerated sense of shame, a premature belief that things will never get better, and an overdeveloped need for achievement at the expense of enjoying the simple wonders of life.

In fact, the only surefire way to *prevent* a comeback in life following misfortune is to commit suicide. Ups and downs occur in everyone's life, and many people who are successful are the people best able to tolerate the occasional setback. Perseverance and faith in yourself are qualities that can inoculate you against depression and suicidality when you encounter hard times.

Something to appreciate about many of the stressful life events we have reviewed here is that crisis periods are usually temporary. It may sound trite to say that "time heals all wounds" or "it is darkest before the dawn," but it is crucial to realize that suicidal feelings usually come at the lowest point. If you can somehow ride out the limited period of time in which you feel your worst, you will survive. You eventually may even prosper. Only the act of suicide makes this positive outcome impossible.

Environmental Factors

As previously stated, it is not negative life events themselves but the beliefs that people maintain about them that account for suicidal reactions. However, no man or woman is an island, and we all are affected by the environment in which we live. Our environment affects us in a variety of ways, including what beliefs we develop and why we hold on to them. Next, we discuss the categories of environmental factors that studies have shown to be associated with suicide risk.

Inadequate Social Support

Many people who become suicidal suffer from a sense of isolation and lack of social support. We generally do not realize the extent to which we rely upon other people and social institutions; but we certainly notice when support from others is absent. Social support comes in many different shapes and forms, including families, religious congregations, employers, friends, and neighbors. Service agencies, such as mental health centers and the YWCA, also fulfill important support functions in the community.

Persons at risk for suicide often exist in environments lacking in social support. Their families might be incapable of offering help and understanding during stressful periods, and often little is to be found when they turn to the community for help. On the other hand, sometimes potential sources of support are there, but negative filtering caused by depression prevents the suicidal individual from seeing them. The resulting feelings of isolation can be difficult to overcome without help. A therapeutic program to develop a social support network is an important part of combating suicidality. We will discuss support systems further in Chapter 5.

Modeling by Parents and Others

To some degree, suicidality runs in families. One reason for this is that certain disorders, such as depression, bipolar disorder, and substance abuse, have a hereditary component. If both of your parents suffered from clinical depression, there is a good chance that you will be susceptible to depression as well.

However, heredity is only part of the picture: If it were the whole story, then all identical twins in the world would always share the same psychiatric disorder, and we know they do not. Our environment plays a big role, and nowhere is that role more pronounced than in the household where we grow up. We learn a great deal about life from our families. We don't just learn behaviors, we learn attitudes as well.

If you witnessed your parents or siblings exhibiting severe, chronic, depressive symptoms, as well as suicidal behaviors, you might well have been influenced by them. This is especially true if one or more of these relatives actually carried a suicide to completion.

It is one of the interesting, yet frustrating, facts of life that we tend to learn and imitate even the things we *dislike* about our families. For example, have you ever shaken your head in dismay after catching yourself in a vulnerable moment sounding "just like Mom"? This also holds true for attitudes about hope, self-worth, self-harm, and others.

If members of your immediate family have been suicidal, it is possible that you have adopted some of their viewpoints. This does not mean that you are doomed to repeat the past. It simply means that you have had powerful learning experiences that need to be counteracted by new learning experiences that are more affirming of yourself, your life, and your future. It means that you will need to be on the lookout for impulsive, self-defeating, and self-harming reactions to stress, because this has become one of your well-learned habits. Fortunately, with some work and encouragement, you can overcome old habits.

Reinforcement of Suicidal Talk and Behaviors

It is a well-known fact in psychology that behaviors that are rewarded tend to be repeated. That is why we praise children when they work hard on their homework, say "thank you" in response to a kind deed, and work harder for incentive pay.

Sometimes, however, negative behaviors and attitudes inadvertently get rewarded. This is most likely to happen in a household in which there is a lack of praise and affection and family members are more likely to get attention if something is wrong or if they get into trouble. In such cases, the negative behavior gets reinforced, because of a lack of reinforcement (reward) of positive behaviors.

For example, we can see how a depressed teenager might resort to threats of suicide in order to get parents' attention. When parents spring into action, but do nothing else to change the nature of the family relationships, they unwittingly reinforce the teenager's tendency to become suicidal in order to get noticed. Similarly, a spouse who feels neglected—that is, until a suicide attempt—may become inclined to engage in suicidal behavior as a primary way to keep the other spouse invested and involved in the marriage.

When these types of problems occur, it is not only the suicidal person who needs professional care but the marital or family unit as well. Everyone involved must learn new ways of interacting so that positive, life-affirming, and relationship-enhancing viewpoints and behaviors are reinforced. Like individual habits, family habits can be hard to break, but the payoff for a positively changed family system can be enormous and well worth the effort.

Romanticization of Suicide: From Romeo and Juliet to Suicide Rock

Another environmental factor that has been known to play a role in propagating faulty beliefs about suicide can be subsumed under the rubric, "the arts and the media." We are not bashing freedom of speech; we are strong proponents of this basic, fundamental right. However, we need to be aware of some of the messages that are sent to people who may be very vulnerable, impressionable, or not optimally aware of the differences between fantasy and the real world.

As an example, let us refer to the politician who killed himself at a press conference in Philadelphia. The event was widely broadcast on television, but some networks had the sensitivity to sacrifice ratings for the sake of decency and safety. They chose not to replay the actual shooting. This is the kind of social responsibility that we applaud, in that there are too many people who otherwise may view such an incident as a way to get their "15 minutes of fame." We have all heard of "copycat killings." Similarly, there are copycat suicides.

In addition, music and literature have played an unfortunate role in making suicide seem "cool" or romantic in some way. This is most apt to happen when the author or artist fails to depict the horror and tragedy inherent in the suicide. In other words, the serious *consequences* are not sufficiently spelled out.

To illustrate our point, we can argue that Shakespeare succeeded in portraying suicide in a responsible manner in *Romeo and Juliet* because the devastating outcome is made apparent to the reader. By contrast, there were a number of highly talented British poets in the early 20th century who inspired their fellow countrymen to go off to the battlefields of World War 1. They glorified the prospect of dying for one's country. While this may be patriotism at its highest level, it is also a slanted and over-romanticized portrayal of death. Interestingly, there was a backlash by other poets, who roundly chastised the "War Poets" and lent their support to life over war.

Today, there has been great debate about the effects of "suicide rock" on young people. Many musicians claim that their lyrics need to be taken in their proper context—that songs about suicide are actually satirical or polemic, and therefore are *against suicide.* Nevertheless, this necessitates clear and objective thinking from the listener. Since we know that people who are severely depressed are prone to negatively biased thinking, the music may actually teach dangerously accepting attitudes toward suicide—for example, that suicide is the best solution to life's problems. This is a very thorny issue, indeed.

4

Not So Fast—Maybe You Don't Need to Change

Suicidal people sometimes express resentment—even outrage—that anyone would presume to advise them not to commit suicide. "Whose life is it anyway?" they ask. "Who are you to tell me that life is worth living when you haven't walked a mile in my shoes?" Well-intentioned family members or therapists often plead with the suicidal individual or demand that he or she not commit suicide, sometimes even resorting to guilt trips or pressure tactics. Frequently, the effect is only to increase the suicidal person's determination to defy those who would try to control him or her.

If we have learned nothing else from our more than 30 combined years of clinical experience, it's that it is silly to assume that people want or need to change. More often in our early years than we like to admit, we worked furiously (and sincerely) trying to "fix" patients, when those very patients sometimes were less committed to change than we were. Why is this important? Simply because the process of psychological change requires belief on the part of the individual that change is worth its cost in terms of the time and effort it requires.

In this respect, emotional healing is very different from many kinds of physical healing. When we have bronchitis or a toothache, we simply go to our physician or dentist and let him or her do *to* us whatever is needed, such as prescribing pills or filling a cavity. Psychological and behavioral change, on the other hand, require commitment and motivation rooted in a strong belief that change is needed and will be beneficial. This is why it is sometimes said (although it's not quite true) that an alcoholic must "hit bottom" before a therapist can be of much help.

We make no assumption that you need to change. It is our philosophical belief that, while it is our job to help you meet your goals to improve your life, it's none of our business to tell you that you should change. Whereas we strongly believe that you will be better off without suicidal thoughts and behaviors, we understand from a practical standpoint that you will only use what we have to offer if you clearly see and believe that working to eliminate your suicidality will be worth the time and trouble.

We therefore propose to approach this, not by attempting to coax or cajole you, but by guiding you through a process similar to one you would follow to make any important decision. Do you remember how you made the best decisions in your life, whether regarding marriage, job, education, or home purchase? In all likelihood, part of your decision-making process was to compare the advantages and disadvantages—pros and cons—of your various options. So let us now consider the respective advantages and disadvantages of attempting or committing suicide.

Advantages of Suicide—Are You Kidding?

Many of our patients are surprised—even shocked—that we are willing to seriously discuss with them reasons *in favor of* their committing suicide. This is understandable, since people who care about them generally have given them nothing but reasons *not* to commit suicide. This is fine, except that failure even to consider the "advantages" of suicide can prevent the decision-making process from ever being completed. Compare this to the reluctant bride who never considers the relative merits of getting married versus staying single. She might go ahead and get married but continue to have lingering doubts about being happier if she had stayed single. On the other hand, seriously considering the advantages of staying single allows her to evaluate those advantages in a realistic light.

When you do this, you often find is that many advantages have at least one "catch." For example, one advantage to being single is being able to date different people. The catch? How about wondering whom to ask out this weekend (and every following weekend); or enduring lousy blind dates; or dealing with questions from relatives about when you're going to "settle down"; or worry about contracting AIDS. Suddenly, all of that freedom begins to look a little different. (Of course, this particular decision cannot be made satisfactorily without considering the advantages and catches to being married as well.)

Similarly, suicidal people sometimes opt to stay alive "for now" but continue to have the lingering idea that perhaps suicide might be the preferable alternative in the long run. This is often because they haven't fully considered the pros and cons. In other words, if you don't take a look at the *plusses* of suicide, you'll never be able to see the "disadvantages to the advantages." Now that you know our agenda, let's forge ahead.

Exercise 3: Exploring the "Advantages" of Suicide

Begin by listing on a sheet of paper all of the advantages of killing yourself that you can think of (hold off for now on any reasons for only attempting or threatening suicide—we'll get to those later). Next, take a look at Table 4-1; it contains a list of often-heard advantages to committing suicide. If you find your plusses in this list, you can discard your own list and just use the table; if any of your own plusses are missing from Table 4-1, add them to the left side in the space provided.

Now shift your attention to the right half of the table and study the catch to each of the supposed advantages of suicide. In the interest of brevity, we have given only one catch per advantage, but you might find that you begin to come up with catches of your own. Add those to the table as well. Finally, move down to any advantages that you added to the left side of Table 4-1 and see what catches come to mind. If none do, we recommend that you consult with a friend or therapist about this, because you're probably overlooking something. For even though we have tried, we have not yet been able to come up with a single advantage to suicide that did not have at least one major catch!

This exercise is meant to show you that the complications of suicide are greater than they appear at first glance. However, you might feel that it misses the mark for you if your suicidality has been such that you were "suicidal" but didn't really want to die (you may have noticed that this fits the pattern of the Communication/Control individual described in Chapter 2). If so, you may feel pressured by others to give up your occasional bouts of suicidal thinking and self-harming behavior but not feel motivated to change. This is the case for many patients, who sometimes get into power struggles with their therapists. Correspondingly, therapists, because they care for their patients and want greatly for them to give up repeated—and often frightening—episodes of suicidal threats and suicide attempts, sometimes inadvertently play into such power struggles.

Again, although we might wish it, we do not expect you to give up something from which you believe you reap a net benefit. Our patients with anger problems are in much the same boat. If they don't get in touch with the *advantages* of their angry behavior (such as often getting their way because they scare people), they are not likely to get in touch with the *disadvantages* that will motivate them to change (such as the fact that people who fear them seldom like them). So let's do essentially the same exercise as before, this time considering the plusses and catches to suicidal thinking and non-fatal self-harming behavior. Remember, this second exercise focuses on the advantages of being suicidal—that is, thinking or talking about killing yourself or actually hurting yourself in suicide attempts—not on actually killing yourself. You can use Table 4-2 for this exercise or make up your own list on a separate sheet of paper.

Table 4-1: The "Plusses" of Suicide

The Plus	The Catch
I'll no longer be a burden to others.	How do I know that my death won't make their burden *greater*?
I'm a failure. At least I'll go out with one success: my death.	By dying I give up all past and possible future successes.
At least I won't hurt anymore.	I'll never feel good anymore, either.
When I'm dead, they'll be sorry for how they treated me.	I won't be around to enjoy my revenge.
This is the one way I can feel in control.	Being dead is the ultimate loss of control.
By killing myself, I will atone for my many sins.	The "punishment" will have no effect on my future behavior, because I'll be dead.
At last, he/she will see how much I loved him/her and will love me in return.	I won't know about this, because I'll be dead.
I'll be happier in the hereafter.	I run the risk that my concept of the hereafter is totally mistaken.
Other Plusses:	**Other Catches:**
_____	_____
_____	_____
_____	_____
_____	_____

Were you able to add to the list of plusses of being suicidal and to identify at least one catch for each? Once again, if you are still convinced that any of the purported benefits of suicidal thinking and acts of self-harm are without major disadvantages, we urge you to discuss this with a therapist or wise friend. To adapt an old saying, "Ten thousand scientists can't be wrong." It's highly unlikely that so many researchers and therapists would be dedicated to eliminating suicidality if the supposed advantages were for real. If you have listed a plus that you think is without a catch, you've probably overlooked something.

Table 4-2: The Plusses of "Being Suicidal"

The Plus	The Catch
This will get them to take me seriously.	What happens when the crisis has passed?
It will get him/her to change his/her ways.	He/she will feel resentful about being coerced; such changes seldom last, anyway.
I want to keep this option, because it's comforting to know that I can always end it if things get too bad to bear.	Keeping suicide "alive" as an option blocks me from fully considering other, possibly more beneficial, options.
This is a powerful way to get even with the people who hurt me.	Retribution usually results in a vicious cycle of hurt and reprisals.
Speaking and acting in suicidal ways is an effective way to get help.	This type of communication often leads to misunderstandings and can result in accidental suicide.
This will finally get across to them how much I really hurt.	This type of communication often leads to misunderstandings and can result in accidental suicide.
Other plusses:	Other catches:
_____	_____
_____	_____
_____	_____
_____	_____

Disadvantages of Suicide—More than Meets the Eye

Effective decision making involves considering both the pros and cons of a decision. Who knows, perhaps the advantages to suicide, however limited, outweigh the disadvantages. So let us now turn to the disadvantages of suicide. In other words, why all the fuss about preventing suicide?

The Illogic of Suicide: Underestimating the Costs

In the early days of the TV program *Saturday Night Live*, Chevy Chase used a running joke in his role as *"Weekend Update"* news anchor, stating each week, in a "news flash," that Generalissimo Francisco Franco was *still dead*. Chase sometimes would go on to say that the Generalissimo's condition "remained stable." One of the things that made this routine morbidly funny was the amazing idea that Franco might become something *other* than dead with each passing week. We all know intellectually that death is final and eternal, and any implication to the contrary is the stuff of fairy tales, horror movies, or dark comedy sketches.

Nevertheless, the sheer awesomeness and incomprehensibility of "forever" prevents us sometimes from fully grasping *just how long death lasts*. Consequently, suicide can look pretty good to a person who is in extreme physical or psychological pain and who, understandably, wishes to obtain relief from his or her suffering. Sadly, this viewpoint puts the suffering individual in danger of pursuing a permanent "solution" to what actually could be a temporary problem.

The problems in living that a suicidal person faces can seem unceasing and interminable. Indeed, to a person in great pain, every minute can feel like an hour, and a day may seem unending. Under these conditions, she or he might turn to suicide as a seemingly reasonable way of escaping from what feels like an eternity of suffering. However, someone in this predicament is likely to be missing some vitally important information that can only be acquired by addressing the following questions:

- Assuming I kill myself, what would have happened for the rest of my natural life had I let myself live?

- How many things—and how many people—will I miss out on if I leave life early?

- How will my suicide affect those I leave behind?

- What exactly will happen to me after I die?

- Will I get another chance at life, or am I about to forfeit my only shot?

- What if I'm wrong in assuming that things will never get better? What will I have done if I kill myself based on a hunch that turned out to be wrong?

- If I kill myself, what kind of legacy will I leave behind? Will I always be remembered as the person who committed suicide and left my loved ones behind? Is this the mark I want to leave on the world?

These are profound questions that can only be answered somewhat speculatively. Still, we wonder how many people who killed themselves actually stopped to consider such questions. When we have asked some of our suicidal patients to ponder these matters, we have heard such answers as, "I don't care anymore," "The answers don't matter," "I don't want to think about it," or "I don't have the energy or the patience for this."

We can summarize our responses to such reactions as follows:

- If you don't care one way or the other, is there any harm or anything to lose in seriously mulling over these issues before taking drastic action?

- If the answers don't matter to you, could you address them nonetheless on the outside chance that the answers you find may matter a great deal to someone else in your life?

- If you don't want to think about it, this is a sign that you are not entirely at peace with your decision to die by your own hand. Do you fear the answers you might come up with, and if so, are you choosing to avoid what you fear? If you're fearful of anything, you haven't truly come to terms with your choice, and you owe it to yourself to work through the issues much more thoroughly, perhaps with the guidance of a trusted other person.

- If you believe that you have neither the energy nor the patience to deal with such questions, consider how little energy you'll have when you're dead and how much patience you'll need to get through eternity if you wrongly choose to die at this time. In comparison, attaining the energy and patience you'll need to sit down and pore over these questions is a piece of cake.

For purposes of illustration, consider the question, "How many things—and how many people—will I miss out on if I decide to leave life early?" If you address this query on a year-by-year basis, you will most likely find that even a summary of what you might miss out on will be an eye-opener.

Over a decade ago, I (CN) posed this question as a therapy assignment to an adolescent client who took a romanticized view of death and professed a wish to kill himself. I asked the client, whom we'll call "Myles," to spell out three or four plausible things that might happen in each of the 60 years following his death and to follow each item with some variant of the statement, "But it won't affect me, because I'll still be dead." I asked Myles to start this assignment in my office, and he spent about 15 minutes generating the following items:

1986: The Yankees win the pennant and Don Mattingly hits 45 home runs. My brother becomes a Bar Mitzvah and my folks throw a big party. My best friend Pat starts a band. But I don't get to see any of this because I'm dead.

1987: I would have been accepted to Columbia and NYU. The Yankees win their second straight pennant. My family goes to visit my aunt and uncle and cousins in Israel. But I don't get to see any of this because I'm still dead.

1988: I would have been a freshman at Columbia. My brother gets interested in a girl but doesn't have a clue and doesn't know who to ask for advice. My friends all drive down to Daytona Beach for spring break. But I don't get to see any of this because I'm still dead.

1989: I would have gotten a great part-time job at NBC studios. I would have met the girl of my dreams at Columbia, but instead she meets someone else. My brother is applying to colleges, and he doesn't have a clue. And none of this has anything to do with me because I'm long gone and getting longer gone every year.

At this point, Myles stopped and said he was tired of it. I reminded him that he had about 56 years of summarizing yet to go. Myles reiterated that he was "bored" with the task. I noted that he had gotten bored in 15 minutes, and wondered aloud how bored he would be for the "15 trillion years or so" that he'd be dead if he were to kill himself. Then I proceeded to expound on the year-by-year list, making up more items about the Yankees, Myles's clueless brother, neat things his friends were doing with their lives, places he would have gone, career possibilities he would have had, and so on, through the 1990s.

Myles began to look exasperated and exclaimed, "Enough already, I get your point!" I retorted, "I don't think you do," and proceeded to do my best fake-it-as-you-go foray into the things that Myles would miss out on in the early twenty-first century. I finally ran out of steam (and ideas) and said:

"Myles, we didn't even get through half of the 60 years, and look at how much you've already missed out on. Yet you seem willing to sacrifice 60 actual years in order to get to a place where you might have trillions of years to kill. Are you beginning to get a sense of the finality of death now? What do you think about this? Do you want to forfeit all of these possible experiences and others to boot?"

The Illogic of Suicide: Underestimating Effects on Others

Now let's turn to the question, "How will my suicide affect those I leave behind?" As you might expect, desperate people who are in pain and thinking of suicide are not in a good position to focus rationally on the feelings of other people. This is not because suicidal people are selfish, but because a suicidal person's emotional pain is so great that there is (at least temporarily) little capacity to consider the feelings of others. It is precisely because of this that anyone who is contemplating suicide needs to sit down and *carefully examine the profound impact that his or her death would have on others.*

You might at first think that this exercise is irrelevant, because you are convinced that no one would miss you if you were gone. This is probably a reflection of depression, which is often characterized by a gross undervaluing of the self. If you think you're not worth anything and don't care about yourself, it stands to reason that you would not expect your friends and relatives to care, either.

Experience has shown us otherwise. In practically all of the cases in which suicidal people maintained this belief, they were, tragically, dead wrong. Others did care about them, but for some reason it didn't register, or it didn't seem believable. As a result, the person who commits suicide loses the chance once and for all of making the most of these relationships. Further, friends and relatives often are left with tremendous guilt, grief, and a void in their lives.

Again, you might think, "This doesn't apply to me. Nobody loves me. Nobody cares." You might even think that others will be better off if you commit suicide. Some people are willing to die for this belief, accepting it as truth, without question. But in the face of such self-destructive extremism, let us ask even more questions:

- How do you *know* that others will be better off if you're dead?

- How can you predict the *long-term* consequences?

- Who has actually told you that they would prefer that you weren't around? In contrast, who has told you that they didn't want you to die and that, in fact, they were worried sick about you?

- Would they really be better off if you were dead, or would they be better off if you were feeling more hopeful and alive again?

- If you have concealed your suicidal thoughts from the important people in your life, why is this? Are you concerned that they would try to stop you from committing suicide? If so, why do you think they would want to stop you? Is this consistent with the notion that they would be better off without you?

- If you think that it will take your committing suicide before people wake up and realize just how much they care, who will benefit from such a scenario? Is there a better way to test and improve the strength of your most important relationships without putting your life on the line?

Sometimes suicidal people are able to acknowledge that other people do care about them and would be hurt by their suicide. However, the suicidal person believes, "They'll get over it." We can state definitively from our work with clients who have lost significant others to suicide that people may learn to live with the reality of a loved one having committed suicide, but they do not simply "get over it." It is not uncommon for us to see people in therapy still grappling with the suicide of a loved one many years after the fact.

Make no mistake about it, you are trivializing the feelings of others and monumentally underestimating your importance in their lives whenever you think that others would not suffer as a result of your suicide. If you are thinking, "But they are suffering with me now. I want to relieve them of their suffering by killing myself," again, ask yourself the question posed earlier: Are they better off with you dead or better off with you alive and more hopeful?

Suicide is not the reasonable solution it sometimes seems to be. *Recovery from depression* is the solution. This may currently seem impossible to you, but it is not. It might take time, effort, new learning, therapy, and perhaps some form of medication, but it can be done. Take the time to ask the important people in your life whether they'd prefer that you take this hopeful route or the hopeless route of self-inflicted death. Just as importantly, ask yourself.

"Now I'm Really Trapped: Suicide Was My Only Way Out, and You've Taken *That* Away."

What thoughts and feelings do you notice yourself having, now that you are nearing the end of this chapter? We hope you are feeling energized by a revised perspective on suicide, one that points away from preoccupation with your own demise and toward new options for yourself. However, because of negative, depressive thinking, you might find yourself feeling as pessimistic as ever. Because the option of suicide can carry with it a sense of security (however false), you might notice feelings of anxiety, sadness, or even anger, as reflected in the heading of this section. The thinking goes something like this: "I've been miserable for what seems like forever; and although I do have mixed feelings about suicide (why else would I be reading this book?), suicide is the only escape in sight from this utter misery that has been my life. Take away my suicide option, and all I have to look forward to is more misery for the rest of my natural life. No, thanks!"

To this we would respond in two ways. First, just as suicide and suicidality have certain advantages and disadvantages, so also does the *absence* of suicide and suicidal behavior. We hope that the advantages to letting yourself live are obvious: seeing your children grow up, reaching career goals, enjoying changes of the seasons, reaping the rewards of retirement, and so on. However, if these are not obvious to you, we urge you to take time now to list your own *advantages to living*, much as you did with the

A classic example of what can happen when people lose sight of their value to those around them was portrayed by James Stewart in the role of George Bailey, in the timeless film *It's a Wonderful Life*. Driven to despair by apparent bankruptcy, frightened by the prospect of going to jail, and condemning himself for the harm that he thought he had caused his family and his clients, George was on the verge of throwing himself off a bridge into an icy river to his death.

As the story goes, George was given a second chance by Clarence, his guardian angel. However, Clarence was smart enough to know that he could not simply cajole George into believing that he was important to many people and that life was worth living. Clarence had to show George firsthand by taking him on a nightmarish journey through time, in which George saw for himself the devastating consequences that would have befallen so many people, loved ones and strangers alike, had he never been born. By the time this fantasy trip had ended, George understood in a way he had never seen before how precious and meaningful his life and his relationships were. The problems that had led him to the brink of suicide no longer mattered as much. George had once again become connected with life.

Though a fictional story, *It's a Wonderful Life* teaches us that we make a grievous error by assuming that our lives do not matter. It reminds us that many people will suffer because of our absence and that our contributions to the lives of others often are difficult to detect and therefore are incalculable.

option of suicide earlier in this chapter. As before, if you have trouble, ask someone to help you add to your list. We also encourage you to refer back to the discussion of reasons for living in the previous chapter.

What about *disadvantages* of giving up the suicide option? There aren't many that we know of, but one is that you might continue to experience periods of emotional distress for a while longer while you are working on your recovery. Here, it is essential to remember that "a while longer" does not equal forever! Such "forever" thinking is indicative of distorted thinking, which brings us to our second point.

We have not yet discussed how to recognize and change errors in thinking that lead to emotional distress (that will be covered in Chapter 7), but go back right now to the end of the first paragraph in this section and see if you can find a cognitive error. What's missing from that line of thinking? If you look closely, you will find a critical *mistaken assumption*, namely, that nothing will ever change. Right now, because of your history, you might believe that this is a correct assumption—why should you expect things to change when life has been bad for so long? The answer is so obvious that you might have overlooked it: *You are about to embark on a systematic, tested strategy of self-change and life improvement*. That's why you have good reason to dispute your assumption that things will never change. And that's why you needn't fear setting aside the option of suicide. The aim is not to give up your only route of escape from misery, but to pursue another road away from misery that will not require you to give up your life in the process.

Let's be blunt about something: *We* know that *you* know that giving up the option of suicide is reversible—you will always have the option of self-destruction available to you. Indeed, this is part of the human condition. However, if efforts to pursue other options (such as therapy) are to succeed, it is absolutely necessary that for now you *remove suicide from active consideration*. Otherwise, the effort and energy you put into your therapy will be seriously compromised. This is a little bit like an Olympic athlete who is only marginally committed to his or her sport, perhaps seriously considering a career in broadcasting instead. This attitude cannot help but affect training negatively.

Psychotherapy researchers now think about the process of change in terms of "readiness for change." One theorist speaks of three stages: the "Complainant," the "Visitor," and the "Consumer." The Complainant is clearly distressed and unhappy with current circumstances but spends most time and energy telling anyone who will listen how bad things are. The Complainant shows little interest in changing things, especially if this requires effort or discomfort on his or her part. The Visitor is interested enough in change to attend a few sessions of therapy, perhaps with a spouse or family member, to "test the waters." An individual at this stage of change is likely to take a passive orientation to change, sometimes hoping that other people will change instead.

The Consumer, on the other hand, has made the decision to make things better. He or she has taken responsibility, much like the ideal athlete or heart patient, to do what it takes to achieve his or her goals. The Consumer is fully prepared to "pay the price" of time and energy to reach these goals and is convinced the benefits will far outweigh the costs.

Which stage rings most true for you? If you're not fully into the Consumer stage at this point, that's okay. The transition from Complainant to Consumer doesn't take place overnight. But it doesn't take place automatically, either. Part of becoming a Consumer is actively working at becoming one. One thing you can do is ask yourself regularly at what level of effort you are currently working and strive to move more toward the Consumer mentality. Something else you can do is to make a *therapy contract with yourself*.

A Therapy Contract with Yourself

Many therapists today use treatment contracts, whether toward goals of losing weight, quitting smoking, or eliminating depression. Such contracts help reduce misunderstandings between the therapist and client by specifying what the goals are and what each person agrees to do in pursuit of those goals. Contracts also help increase commitment to an endeavor, be it a business enterprise or a marriage. Before moving on to the next chapter, we encourage you to study and sign the Therapy Contract with Myself, which appears on the next page.

Some of the items in the contract may feel uncomfortable to you, but we encourage you to give them serious consideration. For example, many suicidal patients have been surprised to learn, when asked, that although they thought they wanted to die, all they really wanted was to end their suffering. When asked whether they would still want to die if the suffering were removed, practically all have emphatically replied, "no."

Making a written commitment, even if only to yourself, might be a difficult step for you. As you contemplate the task, we encourage you to consider this question: What do you have to lose? What you stand to lose when following the alternative option (suicidality) is nothing less than your life. The only thing that you stand to lose in the Therapy Contract is time and effort, and you stand to gain much, much more. Doesn't this seem a reasonable risk to take?

A Therapy Contract with Myself

As part of my commitment to myself and my happiness, I endorse the following:

- I proclaim that my goal is not to die, but to take care of my pain.

  _____ (Initial)

- To state it positively: I proclaim that my goal is to live a long, pleasurable life, with less unhappiness than I now experience.

  _____ (Initial)

- I realize that the tendency to become suicidal when depressed or upset prevents me from achieving this goal, whereas overcoming my suicidality will help me reach it. I therefore promise myself to work on learning better ways than suicidality to manage my emotional distress.

  _____ (Initial)

- I hereby declare that I am worth the time and effort it will take to achieve these goals (or: I commit to work on believing that I am "worth it").

  _____ (Initial)

- Because my recovery will take time, I commit in the meantime to resist any urges to injure or kill myself.

  _____ (Initial)

- If at any time I should feel unable to resist impulses to hurt or kill myself, I promise to follow steps outlined in Chapter 5, "Step One: Survive the Crisis."

  _____ (Initial)

I promise myself to abide by the terms of this contract and agree that I will not break the contract until and unless I have discussed this with a therapist or other trusted person who is acting in my best interest.

_____ / _____

Your Signature/Date

PART II

What You Can Do

5

Step One: Survive the Crisis

Suicide is forever. *Feeling* suicidal generally is temporary or intermittent. It is a terrible feeling, as you know, to experience this kind of emptiness and pain. However, this experience tends to fluctuate, even though it may seem to last forever when you are in its depths. The sense that there is no way out—short of killing yourself—is an illusion, a cruel hoax. There is, in fact, a very simple way out. It is the passage of time.

We are not suggesting that the only thing you can do is sit around, wait, and hope against hope that you will start to feel better sometime soon. Rather, you must participate actively in the passage of time. In other words, there are steps you can take to ride out the times when you feel at your lowest points. By taking such steps, you may prevent yourself from doing the one thing (suicide) that no amount of time can ever undo.

In this chapter, we will introduce you to three main strategies that you can use to get through a suicidal crisis. Such strategies will enable you to "make it to the other side," without hurting yourself. We must emphasize that these techniques are only a starting point in your attempts to help yourself to reinvest in your life. They will not solve your problems (we hope to help you to do that in later chapters). Instead, they will assist you in resisting irreversible impulses during your most vulnerable times. They will help you to reach another day, when you will be more willing and able to fight to restore meaning and purpose to your life and diminish your pain.

Delaying Impulses

In a nutshell, this is what delaying impulses is all about: You want to become the all-time champion procrastinator of suicide. Yes, you may plan to commit suicide, but you'll just keep putting it off. Other activities, obligations, and unexpected obstacles will keep getting in the way. Suicide may sound like an attractive option in theory, but in practice it will be too involved, require too much planning and preparation, and will be a huge bother just getting started. So you will put it off, convinced that you'll "get around to it" someday. Any deadlines you may have set (and we apologize for the morbidly poor choice of words here) will pass, and you will still be alive. You will have succeeded in procrastinating once again. Excellent. Let life keep getting in the way of your plans to die.

Delaying Impulses at the Moment of Crisis

The first step in "procrastinating" your attempt at suicide is to delay acting on the desire to harm yourself at the peak of your feelings of despair. Sometimes this may last only one night, or even one hour, though it may seem like an eternity. This is the time you are most apt to harm yourself, but it is also the time you are least able to make a fair-minded decision about what should happen to you. If life has not been fair to you, you owe it to yourself to be fair to yourself and wait until your emotions subside so you can think more clearly. If you believe that suicide itself is a "fair" option, perhaps because you feel you deserve no better, then at least wait until some time has passed so that you can weigh your choices more carefully. Feelings of "deservingness" are very subjective and can easily be distorted by depressed moods. You must give yourself every benefit of the doubt, because suicide can't be undone.

What are some things you can do to ride out the immediate impulse to hurt yourself? The answers are both very simple and very difficult. They are simple because the tasks themselves are fairly ordinary. On the other hand, it takes courage, self-control, and the ability to endure pain to carry them out. Therefore, any efforts on your part to enact these strategies are worthy of admiration.

One such strategy is to get some healthy sleep. Death has been called "The Big Sleep." We suggest you try "the little sleep" first. If you are in need of a temporary escape from pain, sleep is an excellent option. This is particularly true when life has you feeling worn down or when you feel at the end of your rope. Sleep is restorative and can help diminish your pain, buying you some time to think things through more carefully. If you cannot sleep, for whatever reason, do not force the issue. Instead, try another strategy.

Talk to somebody. Regardless of the time of day or night, talk to somebody. Do not die alone. Connect with someone, and live. Choose someone whom you admire and trust. Choose people who have shown their caring in the past. Pick up the phone and make the call. Pay them a visit if they live nearby. Contact them via your home computer, if that is what works for you, but do not suffer alone.

If you are worried about bothering the other person, perhaps because it is late at night, there are other options. First, if you have a therapist, call him or her. A therapist will want to know if you are feeling suicidal. If you do not have a therapist, or if you cannot reach him or her, there are people you can call who are trained to deal with suicidality. Your local Suicide Prevention hotline is a good place to start. They are in the phone book, so keep the number handy.

If you have already taken action against yourself, such as ingesting pills or cutting yourself, you must get to the nearest hospital emergency room as soon as possible. Do not rely on yourself to get there. Call the operator, the police, 911, an ambulance—whomever you can call in an emergency situation—and tell them where you are. Tell them exactly what you have done and how long ago you did it. We hope that you will never have to do this. We hope that you will never actually make a suicide attempt. However, if you do, getting emergency treatment at a hospital will buy you precious time.

Exercise 4: Long-Term Strategies for Delaying Suicidal Impulses

Even when you are not at your lowest point, you may still find yourself making general plans to commit suicide. At such times, we suggest that you do Exercise 4. In this task, reflect on the things you have been meaning to do in (and with) your life that you have either not gotten around to or not completed—in essence, a procrastination list. Generate as many items as possible. Do not list "suicide" as a response until you have exhausted all other possibilities.

This is not to make you feel even worse by focusing on all the things you haven't done. Rather, the purpose is to show you just how much unfinished business you have in your life. All of us, fallible human beings that we are, fail at times to follow through with our plans and best intentions. Procrastination is nothing to be ashamed about, because we all do it.

Next, ponder (and write down) the reasons that each of the items on the procrastination list (up to, but not including, suicide) has been important to you. Of course they are important, otherwise you never would have intended to do them in the first place. Similarly, you never would have chastised yourself for putting them off if they were not important in some way.

Now that you have graphically reminded yourself of the many things that you wish you had done but never got around to, choose one to begin now. For example, if there is a book you always meant to read but never purchased, go out and buy it today. Start reading. Then consider what your next goal will be. If there is a trip you always wanted to take, but never followed through, start planning it today. Call a travel agent, or get information from your auto club. Set up your life so that you simply must delay your plans for suicide, because you have something else more immediate and pressing to do first. As the late, great George Burns once said, "I can't afford to die—I'm booked."

Exercise 4: Unfinished Business in My Life

Things I Have Been Meaning to Do or Complete

1.

2.

3.

4.

5.

6.

7.

Why It Is Important for Me to Live to Do These Things

1.

2.

3.

4.

5.

6.

7.

Unfinished Business I Will Attend to Now

1.

2.

3.

Each time you enact one of your ideas, think of another to take its place, just in case there are future suicidal crises with which to contend. Keep focusing on the idea that having unfinished business in life is good, because it gives you purpose and goals to pursue. Let suicide be the final frontier for procrastination. All other tasks on which you have procrastinated in your life must be attended to first.

You might ask, "What if I exhaust my list and reach the 'suicide' item? Should I then commit suicide?" The answer is no, for the following reasons: If you do this exercise fully and in the proper spirit, your participation in all of these activities and goals will bond you more strongly to life. You will have a greater sense of purpose, meaning, and enthusiasm. You will have begun the all-important process of reinvesting in your life and in your future. You will be less likely to want to die. Also remember that this is only one of many possible strategies to help you get through rough periods and strengthen your connection to life. Your life must not hinge on the effectiveness of this or any other single strategy. Everyone is different; and if one approach doesn't help, something else probably will. Here and throughout this book, persistence will be your most important ally.

If you feel that this exercise asks too much of you or takes too long, it is okay to take it one step at a time. Just start with the procrastination list. Or do one of the suggested activities on the list. The purpose is simply to put off suicide in favor of "other projects" that you might otherwise have left unfinished. Remember, if you decide against suicide, and if you take good care of yourself, you have the rest of your life to do the things that you have always wanted to do. Let the rest of your life be expansive and filled with possibilities, not shortened by suicide.

More Delaying Tactics

Another way to help yourself survive a suicidal crisis is simply to make it very difficult to kill yourself. To start, safeguard your environment. If you own a gun, sell it or turn it over to someone outside your household. If you possess substantial quantities of medication, consult with your doctor about maintaining the necessary medications and their dosages, and discard the rest. If you have alcohol or other psychoactive drugs lying around the house, get rid of them. Suicide is too easy when guns, pills, and alcohol are readily available. Make your environment unfriendly to suicide. This will buy you some valuable time to get through the low periods unharmed.

The next strategy for resisting the impulse to kill yourself is especially applicable when you are convinced that something terrible is going to happen soon, and by committing suicide you will be able to avoid it. If you feel the urge to kill yourself because you foresee terrible things—divorce, bankruptcy, legal troubles, public humiliation, or serious illness—simply refuse to lie down and die. You could be incorrect in your assumption that these awful things will happen or that you will be forever devastated by them. If you can keep yourself alive a little while longer, and then a little while longer still, you might come to find that your worst fears were unfounded. The urge to die will subside. You will discover that it would have been an utter waste to have killed yourself, because you would not have spared yourself anything you couldn't handle.

In essence, your mission is to refuse to be the one who seals your own fate. Play it out as long as you can, and see for yourself if your fears come to pass. If you fear that circumstance and bad luck will prevail, see how long you can forestall these foes. Don't give assistance to the Fates. Defy them as long as you can.

This principle is illustrated in the final act of Shakespeare's *Romeo and Juliet*. Upon finding what he thinks is the lifeless body of his beloved Juliet, Romeo hastily kills himself, believing that all is lost and all he has to live for is gone. Moments later, Juliet awakens from her potion-induced "death." We learn that if Romeo had been able to delay his impulse to destroy himself, he would have been reunited with his love. Instead, both Romeo and Juliet end up victims of impulsive suicide.

This is fiction, of course, but it shows the tragic consequences of a life taken before crucial assumptions are tested. We urge you to adopt the following important rule for your life: *Never make a major, life-altering decision when you are at an emotional extreme*. We cannot emphasize the importance of this principle enough. Many people have damaged or lost their lives because they let negative emotions make their most important decisions for them. A time of emotional turmoil is the absolute worst time to take life-altering action.

You owe it to yourself to do whatever you can to ride out the impulse to kill yourself, at least until you can think and discuss the matter with calmness and serenity. Even then, it is vital that you do all that you can to help yourself, solve your problems, and consult with other people. This brings us to our next strategy for surviving the crisis: involving other people.

Making Use of Your Social Supports

Suicidal states typically carry with them an almost indescribable sense of aloneness. People caught up in this state generally feel alone with their pain, believing that nobody understands or cares. This is another example of drawing a conclusion with a broken heart, without benefit of objective evidence. People who feel alone in the world almost always overlook people who do care for them and who would try to help if given the opportunity. As therapists, we have heard distraught family members, now in therapy themselves, tell us through their tears, "I would have done something to help him, if he had only told me how he felt." The bottom line is this: If you are on the verge of suicide, you need to remember that there is someone out there who wants to know and who will be eager to help if you allow it.

Perhaps you are concerned about burdening others with your problems. If so, think about the burden those who care about you will feel after you are gone, believing they could have done something to help you. Or perhaps you feel it would be humiliating to tell others that you are feeling suicidal. If this is the case, ask yourself why you feel this way. Is it because you fear they will not understand? Give them a chance. If someone you choose to tell doesn't "get it," try someone else. You may be surprised to find someone who was once suicidal himself or herself and, therefore, very much in tune with what you are going through. So many people have felt suicidal at one time or another that this coincidence is very much a possibility, if you only allow yourself to speak to someone about your despair.

If you worry that by sharing your suicidal feelings you will become stigmatized and labeled, we suggest the following: (1) choose someone who seems to be an open-minded thinker; someone in your life who is fair and trustworthy, whether he or she is a friend, relative, colleague, mentor, or therapist; (2) keep in mind that most people respond to suicidality with concern, not criticism, and that most people are not like the stereotypical bystander who urges the person on the ledge to jump to his or her death; and (3) consider the "stigma" of being someone who has *completed* a suicide. While it is true that suicide is not nearly the scandal it was decades ago, it is still a powerful, negative legacy—much more so than if you have thoughts of suicide but never translate them into action.

Another reason that you may hesitate to contact someone when you are contemplating suicide is the thought that "they have heard it all before, and I'm sure they're sick and tired of my problems by now." This is dangerously presumptuous. Just because you dislike and have lost tolerance for yourself does not mean that others share your punitive stance.

On the other hand, your concern for others being "tired of my problems" shows that you have some empathy for their difficult position. It is, after all, quite distressing for people to be in the presence of someone they care for who perhaps soon may die, especially if they feel there is little they can do to change the suicidal person's mind for the better. Our suggestion, therefore, is use your empathy as a strength in this situation. Tell others how much you appreciate their attempts to listen and to be there for you in your time of desperation. Emphasize that you realize you are causing them some distress and that you do not wish to do this. Let them know that you hope to be able to repay their kindness someday (of course, you have to remain alive in order to do this).

Yet another deterrent to your choosing to talk to someone about your suicidal thoughts may be a sense that you will not be taken seriously, so "what's the point?" The point is this: If one person minimizes how you feel, another person may not. If someone is skeptical (for example, responds by telling you that you can't really be serious, or you wouldn't be talking about it, you would "just do it"), you do not need to make the actual suicide attempt to prove your point. Instead, you need to find someone else to talk to. Find someone who is more sympathetic and perhaps more knowledge-able about suicidality.

If you are adamantly opposed to sharing your suicidal thoughts and feelings with other people, you can still benefit from reaching out to others. Instead of feeling alone, and instead of engaging in any self-harming behaviors, seek out other people with whom to share your time. Call someone. Write a letter. Arrange to have dinner with some friends. Visit someone you haven't seen for a while. If you are employed, interact with your coworkers. If you have a difficult time establishing contact with others on a given day, spend some quality time with your dog or cat. Connect. Don't die alone—live with, and amongst, others. Let others be your lifeline, even if only as a temporary measure until you can help yourself, and even if the other people do not realize they are serving in this capacity for you.

Exercise 5: Identifying People Who Care

To practice using your social support system, try Exercise 5. This exercise can be used anytime, but it is particularly useful if you believe that you are all alone and that it is useless to let anyone else know how you feel.

The first step is to write the names of everyone with whom you have some sort of current relationship. The list should include anyone who:

has spoken to you within the past few weeks and knows your name, or

knows your address, phone number, or birthday, or

has complimented you recently, or

has sent you a letter or called recently, or

would likely be deeply saddened on learning of your death, or

would be happy to hear from you because it has been a long time since you last spoke or spent time together, or

you have kissed, hugged, or told, "I love you" within recent memory.

See how many people fit one or more of these criteria. Don't censor your list by making any judgments such as: "This person doesn't count because . . ." Do not quit working on the list because your depression makes you too tired to think or concentrate. As in the movie *Schindler's List*, keep adding to it, adding to it some more, and thinking, "The list is life."

The second step is to write down at least one friendly or otherwise positive interaction you have had with each person. Now put a star by the names of those persons with whom you have had the most recent positive contacts or with whom you have the most rewarding communication. The subsequent steps in the exercise will pertain to these "stars."

Your third step is to reflect on whether each of these persons knows about your depression or suicidality. If you have discussed your feelings with a particular person, decide whether the person seems to have some understanding of what you are going through, and indicate this in the third column of the form. For each person on the list, consider whether he or she has asked, "How are you doing?" in a caring manner lately. Has he or she gone out of his or her way to speak to you or spend time with you? Has the person offered to "help out" or requested that you tell them "if you ever need anything?" Any person who fits this bill is practically begging you to open up and talk. Respect this request and take hold of their helping hand.

Exercise 5: Utilizing Social Support		
Person's Name	**Positive Interactions**	**Knows How I Feel?** (Yes/No/Maybe)

If you believe that few or no people have been aware of your distress, it is possible that you are not picking up on their signs of caring. Or it is possible that they are aware of your negative state of mind but are respecting your right to privacy until you take the initiative to ask for a sympathetic ear. It is also conceivable that you have been maintaining a public demeanor that looks pleasant and composed, therefore people around you have no clue to your level of need for social support. If any of these explanations sounds plausible, it is time to pay closer attention to the signals you are putting out to others, as well as to the signs of caring others are offering to you. Do not hide or close your eyes. Be yourself, and give others the chance to show their support.

Remember, you may not have to tell anyone you are considering suicide (though we suggest that you consider it). It may be sufficient just to let someone know you have been feeling "down" and that you could really use some moral support, understanding, and maybe some time together. Do not be alone with your pain. It has been said that by relating to other people we can "multiply our joys, and divide our pain." Test this theory in your own life, ideally with more than one person.

The fourth and final step in the exercise is to choose one or two people with stars next to their names and *contact them*, at least to spend some time together, but perhaps for a heart-to-heart chat. You can choose a group of people with whom to spend time, if that will make it less threatening. Ultimately, make use of any and all social support that is available to you, whether it is in your personal life, work life, or your therapy life (for example, 12-step groups or your individual therapist). By connecting with all of the "stars" on your list, you will benefit from a full range of social support. You also will guard against becoming overly dependent on any one person and help others to be part of your "team for life." You will be helping yourself and making it more reasonable for others to help you as well.

Finding Ways to Nurture Yourself

The first two strategies for getting through periods of suicidal crisis have involved using the passage of time and seeking support from others. The third strategy is finding ways to take care of *yourself*, especially when feeling upset. You might find this easier said than done, especially if you are low on energy and not feeling kindly toward yourself. Nevertheless, the strategy of self-nurturing, or "self-soothing" is too fundamental a skill to neglect. Because you are available to yourself at any time, you are potentially your own most valuable resource. This strategy essentially says, "I will not abandon myself in my time of need." Others might have previously abandoned you at critical times in your life, but you need not check out on yourself as well. You can be there for yourself.

Lets look at some practical ways do this, beginning with some basics of self-care. Depressed people often neglect to sustain themselves in ways that are necessary for a sense of well-being. This is manifested in problem habits such as not eating well, going to bed at irregular hours, not getting washed or dressed, and rejecting needed medications. These habits are guaranteed to make a depressed person feel even more depressed and lead to more problem behaviors. This is a classic case of the vicious cycle.

For every vicious cycle, there is a positive feedback loop just waiting to get started. If you can start to take a little better care of yourself, even if that means simply going to bed and getting up at reasonable hours or taking a shower and getting nicely dressed, that will begin a positive chain reaction in your life. It's simple, but it works.

In practice, however, this may be difficult for you to do. Depression can make a person lose interest in himself or herself. Do you notice such an apathy about yourself? If so, then you are probably stuck in the vicious cycle. To get out of it, you must be willing to push yourself. You have to be willing to do the small, routine things that are necessary for you to look and feel better. You may think this will do no good, but try it anyway. There is nothing to lose, and you may be surprised.

Another way to self-nurture is to provide yourself with "creature comforts" when feeling upset. Dr. Marsha Linehan (1993) recommends soothing each of the five senses: For vision, you might look at beautiful pictures in a book; for hearing, you can listen to soothing music; for smell, burn a scented candle; for taste, drink herbal tea; and for touch, stroke your pet or cuddle a stuffed animal.

Of course, you cannot expect such activities as these to totally change your life or serve as long-term solutions to your problems. However, they will break the vicious cycle of harmful self-care habits and set a new tone for you to treat yourself better. They will alleviate your distress, at least temporarily, to help you ride out the suicidal crisis or get help.

Finally, don't forget that self-soothing also includes your active use of the antisuicide techniques presented in this book. By helping yourself, you will feel better, more in control, and proud of yourself for having the courage to persist under adverse conditions. Your hard work and newly acquired skills will translate into a sense of satisfaction and well-being. These skills represent the highest level of self-soothing, because they teach you to think, feel, and act as your own therapist.

6

Step Two: Know Thyself
(Thinking and Feeling)

"Meanings are not determined by situations, but we determine ourselves by the meanings we give to situations."

—Alfred Adler

Thinking and Feeling

We come now to what is perhaps the most hopeful (and therefore antisuicidal) idea in this book: YOU CAN CHANGE HOW YOU FEEL. Before we tell you how, we must first show you how feelings such as depression and despair are created. To illustrate, consider the following tale:

> An old farmer was tilling his fields when his 6-year-old grandson came running toward him with wide eyes. "Grampa, Grampa! Come quick! Bobby and Betty Sue are fixin' to pee in the hay!" "What?" replied the old farmer, hearing the words but unable to comprehend the meaning. "I said, Come quick! Bobby and Betty Sue are fixin' to pee in the hay!" Still perplexed, the farmer thought it best to buy some time. "Son, I think you'd better tell me exactly what you saw," he said. "Well," the boy replied, "All's I know is they was kissin' and huggin' in the loft, and then they started pullin' down their pants, and that's when I came runnin to you 'cause I could see they was fixin' to pee in the hay!" "Son," the wizened farmer said with a smile, "You got the facts straight, but I'm afraid you've drawed the wrong conclusion."

As often is the case in human affairs, humor shows us important truths. Although growing into adulthood helps clear up many of life's mysteries (sex, for example), in no way do we at age 21 suddenly become immune from "drawing the wrong conclusion." As therapists, we see this every day: Good, decent people tell us that they are worthless—failures at life!—because they became unemployed, were rejected by a loved one, or made mistakes at parenting. As in our story about the farmer and his grandson, they often get the facts straight but draw the wrong conclusions. And, unlike in the story, the consequences of these misinterpretations are serious, even life endangering. Clinical depression and suicidal thoughts and behaviors almost always occur in the context of such erroneous ideas.

This simple but profound principle—that disturbed emotion is produced and maintained largely by erroneous thinking—forms the basis of the "cognitive revolution" in clinical psychology, psychiatry, and counseling. From Aaron T. Beck's Cognitive Therapy to Albert Ellis's Rational-Emotive Therapy, advances by cognitive therapists and researchers have done more to increase the effectiveness of psychotherapy than perhaps any development since Sigmund Freud first described the unconscious or B. F. Skinner showed how rewards and punishments influence behavior.

To set the stage for learning how to feel better by changing depressive thinking, lets review three key principles from the science and theory of cognitive therapy:

1. *Negative emotions such as depression and anxiety are fueled in large measure by identifiable negative thoughts and cognitive distortions.* An immense body of research supports this principle. For example, psychologist Martin Seligman at the University of Pennsylvania has shown that depressed people have a clear tendency to blame themselves for bad events, whereas nondepressed people tend to attribute similar events to temporary states or situations. A depressed person might explain a low test score by thinking, "I'm stupid," whereas a nondepressed individual might attribute such a disappointment to the difficulty of the test or to not having studied hard enough. It's not hard to see which interpretation would tend to make a depression worse.

There are many other ways that thinking errors contribute to depression; we'll get to these in detail a little later.* Suffice it to say that, contrary to how you may feel, emotional misery is not created solely by influences beyond your control.

Please don't misunderstand. This does not mean that you deliberately create your own suffering. Although Freud and some of his followers main-

---

* We are not suggesting that depression is "caused" by erroneous thinking. Depression and other psychological disorders are caused by a collection of biological, environmental, and learned factors. However, depression most definitely is aggravated and maintained by depressive thinking; and depression gets better when these thinking patterns change.

tain that some people have a "need to suffer," we most emphatically reject this notion for the vast majority of suicidal people. Rather, evidence suggests that people unintentionally make themselves miserable by buying into unrealistically negative beliefs about themselves and their world.

2. *Depressive thinking patterns, while usually outside of a persons awareness, can be brought into awareness fairly readily.* If as you read this you find yourself thinking, "I don't have any thoughts that make me depressed; the feeling just grabs me," this is normal. Most of our thinking, including depressive thinking, is unconscious or "automatic." For example, do you remember thinking about tying your shoes this morning or telling yourself how to brush your teeth? The good news, however, is that thinking patterns can be discovered quickly, and certainly without years and years of therapy. In fact, you've probably become aware of some of your own depressive thoughts while reading this book.

3. *Depressive and suicidal thinking patterns, when brought into awareness, can be changed; and changed thinking leads to changed emotions.* Consider the example of the low test score mentioned earlier. It stands to reason that if the depressed person can learn to interpret such an event more like the nondepressed individual, that person will feel less depressed. In fact, this is exactly what we find in practice and exactly what a mountain of research evidence supports. Did you know that a collection of very rigorous studies have shown that cognitive therapy works as well as antidepressant medications? Some studies suggest that cognitive therapy actually works better, in that it has staying power even after therapy has ended.

In any event, what's important to know for the purposes of this book is that *you can learn to recognize and change the erroneous thoughts that fuel your depressive feelings and suicidal impulses.* So let's take a look at how you can begin.

Suicidal Thinking: Cognitive Distortions and 17 Dangerous Beliefs

The first step in recognizing and changing your pain-producing thoughts is to learn a little bit about thought processes in general and then about suicidal thinking in particular. Let's begin with a simple but profound principle: *A thought is not a fact.* Obvious statement, you might think. Anyone knows that simply thinking a thought such as "I am fabulously wealthy" does not suddenly swell your bank account and land you on *Lifestyles of the Rich and Famous.* But consider other thoughts that may sound more familiar— thoughts such as "I'm so stupid," "No one gives a damn," or "The future is hopeless." These are all thoughts which carry the weight (and pain) of truth but seldom hold much water when put to the test.

Take "John," for example, a high-school principal and father of two, who came in for treatment of his depression and increasingly frequent suicidal thoughts. When asked about reasons for his low spirits, John replied, "I feel like a failure. I'm not much of a father, and I'm constantly fearful at work that I will be exposed as a fraud. My Dad always said I wouldn't amount to anything, and he was right."

With thoughts like these, it was not surprising that John was depressed. But when we began examining the reality of his life, it became more and more clear that John's beliefs were not consistent with the "facts." John had his share of shortcomings as a father, but he was much beloved by his sons, as well as by his wife of many years. And despite his deep doubts about his adequacy at work, he had functioned effectively at work for years and had, in fact, been formally recognized on several occasions for exemplary performance.

Cognitive therapists would say that John's thinking was "distorted," and these distortions probably were caused by, and contributed to, his depression. In no sense did John bring these thoughts on deliberately, nor did his distortions reflect any lack of intelligence on his part. Rather, when faced with evidence contrary to the inadequate self-image he had learned as a child, John unknowingly fell into distorting the facts to fit them into his sense of self, rather than changing his self-image to fit reality. Through therapy, he was able to reverse this process and began to appreciate and enjoy his accomplishments.

One of Aaron T. Beck's most enduring contributions to cognitive therapy has been his explanation of various ways that people's thinking becomes distorted. Here is a list and brief description of each distortion, as described by Dr. David Burns (for a more thorough discussion, we recommend Dr. Burns's book, *Feeling Good*):

- All-or-nothing thinking: You see things in black-and-white categories. For example, if your performance is not perfect, you see yourself as a total failure.

- Overgeneralization: You see a single negative event as a never-ending pattern of defeat.

- Mental filter: You pick out a single negative detail and dwell on it exclusively, so that your vision of all of reality becomes darkened.

- Disqualifying the positive: You reject positive experiences by insisting they "don't count," thereby maintaining a negative worldview despite evidence to the contrary.

- Jumping to conclusions: You make a negative interpretation even though there are no definite facts that convincingly support your conclusion. Jumping to conclusions takes two forms. In *mind reading*, you assume that people are thinking bad things, but you have no valid evidence to that effect. In *fortune-telling*, you make negative predictions about the future without realizing that your predictions may be inaccurate.

- Magnification or minimization: You exaggerate the importance of negative things (such as your mistakes) or shrink positive things (such as your accomplishments) until they disappear.

- Emotional reasoning: You assume that negative emotions necessarily reflect the way things really are ("I feel hopeless, therefore it must be true").

- Shoulds, musts, and oughts: You try to motivate yourself with shoulds and shouldn'ts, as if you had to be whipped and punished before you could be expected to do anything.

- Labeling: This is an extreme form of overgeneralization. Instead of describing your error, you attach a negative label to yourself, such as, "I'm a loser."

- Personalization: You see yourself as the cause of some negative external event which in fact you were not primarily responsible for.

You might be surprised to see how many ways there are to "draw the wrong conclusion!" Be careful not to personalize or overgeneralize this information by telling yourself that you're crazy or totally beyond help. For years Albert Ellis pointed to the volumes of research showing that *all* human beings seem to have an inborn tendency toward "crooked thinking." Fortunately, it's not necessary to rid ourselves totally of all irrational thinking— indeed, to insist on perfect rationality would be irrational. What we can do is learn to recognize and change those distortions that have the most negative impact on us. Let's take a look at a few examples now.

Exercise 6: Identifying Cognitive Distortions

In a pioneering book on cognitive therapy of depression, published in 1979, Aaron T. Beck and colleagues showed how depression involves negative thinking in three areas: negative view of self, negative view of the world, and negative view of the future. He referred to this as the "negative cognitive triad." Exercise 6 lists "17 Dangerous Beliefs" that fall under these headings, plus a few spaces to write any beliefs of your own that you notice when feeling suicidal. In the space opposite each belief, see if you can identify which cognitive distortions are represented by each belief. The answers to Exercise 6 are given at the end of the chapter.

How did you do? Whether you did well or poorly, use the occasion to examine what you are feeling and thinking about the exercise itself. If you did well and you are feeling pleased, pay attention to what encouraging words you might be saying to yourself to create this feeling of satisfaction. (Remember, it is not your *performance* that is making you feel good; for no matter how well you did, it would still be possible for you to discourage

Exercise 6: 17 Dangerous Beliefs

Dangerous Belief	Cognitive Distortion(s)
Beliefs about Self	
I'm inadequate and a loser.	
I can't stand the pain.	
I'm so bad, this is what I deserve.	
If I want something very much, then I can't live without it.	
I just can't cope like other people.	
Beliefs about Others and the World	
Hurting myself is the only way I can get what I need from others.	
No one would miss me if I were gone.	
They'll be better off without me.	
They'll be sorry.	
Life's a bitch and then you die.	
Hurting myself is the only way to feel better.	
Beliefs about the Future	
This life will never give me what I need.	
I'll never be loved.	
The next life will be better.	
The future holds nothing for me but pain.	
Self-harm is my best or only option.	
I have no reason to go on.	
Thoughts of Your Own When Feeling Suicidal	

yourself by telling yourself its "no big deal" (see "Minimization" in the list of distortions) or that you "should" have done better (see "Shoulds, musts and oughts").

If you didn't do so well and you are feeling discouraged, what thoughts are making you feel that way? Write these thoughts down and determine whether they contain any of the distortions contained in our list. Don't worry about correcting the distortions right now—well get to that later. For now, just practice telling yourself, "That's only a negative thought; and a thought is not necessarily a fact."

Learning from Moods and Pain

This section will help you learn how to observe your moods. Although you may think you know exactly how you feel and when you feel it, you will be surprised how much you can learn and benefit from recording what you are thinking and feeling. Just as we use scales in weight-loss programs rather than relying on how heavy we "feel" today, it is important to try to be somewhat objective about how we feel emotionally.

Consider this question: When reflecting on your life, does your unhappiness seem constant, unremitting? Do you find yourself thinking, "I am depressed all the time—100 percent miserable 100 percent of the time." If so, you have all the more reason to learn to observe your moods; for however much you might believe you are "always" unhappy, it is practically impossible to feel exactly the same way, all day, every day, without any fluctuations. Even when life is severely problematic and painful, at least minicycles of ups and downs do occur. The same principle applies to wishes to live or die: Subtle changes in mood, thought, and action occur over time. Becoming aware of these experiential shifts can present you with a vital window of opportunity to learn some important things about controlling your moods and suicidal impulses, rather than being controlled by them.

One of the first steps you can take is to *learn* from your moods, whether they're good, bad, or somewhere in between. In order to do this, you must try to observe yourself as if you were an outside observer—a scientist, if you will.

Most moods and behaviors result from a three-component process, consisting of a triggering event, an interpretation of the event, and resultant feelings and behaviors. The process looks something like this:

Trigger event ⟶ Interpretation ⟶ Feeling/behaviors

If this model seems familiar, it should; for we have been making use of it throughout this chapter. It is the cornerstone of cognitive therapy, and its implications are nothing short of revolutionary. What it means is that, contrary to how things may seem, human beings are not at the mercy of things that happen to them.

Let's return to your reaction to the cognitive distortion exercise. Suppose you didn't do so well with it and ended up feeling upset and discouraged and lit up a cigarette. Your first reaction might have been to experience your upset as having been caused by your less-than-wished-for performance. But now you can develop a more sophisticated (and therapeutic) understanding of what went on. Before you read any further, see if you can identify the three components of your reaction in the space below or on a separate piece of paper:

Trigger event: _____

My interpretation: _____

Feelings/behaviors: _____

As you probably were quick to determine, the trigger event was not doing as well as you'd hoped on the exercise, and the feelings/behaviors were upset, discouragement, and lighting a cigarette. Now, here's the hard part, for most of our thinking about events is silent (unconscious) and generally passes unnoticed. In addition, thinking is about as different from one person to another as anything can be, so we can't provide one correct answer to the exercise. Here are a few possible interpretations that could account for feeling upset and discouraged following a disappointment or failure:

This is too hard; I'll never get it.

I'm so stupid!

There it is: more proof that I'm a failure.

If I can't do this, I must be beyond help.

I can't stand this frustration—I need a cigarette.

Do you recognize a few cognitive distortions here? Do the feelings resulting from this trigger event begin to make sense given such discouraging thoughts? Can you see how if you said such things to another person (and they believed you) they would feel the same way? Can you see how suicidal thoughts would not be far behind, such thoughts as, "I must be beyond help"?

Now, let's try an experiment. In the space below, write several new interpretations of the same trigger event. For guidance, imagine that you are talking to the person you care most about in the world who experienced a similar disappointment and was feeling miserable about it. Vividly picture this son, daughter, spouse, lover, or friend in the room and feeling intense pain. What would you say?

New interpretations:

_____

_____

_____

How did you do? Here are a few examples of constructive, rather than discouraging, interpretations of a failure experience:

I'm sorry you didn't do well, but I'm glad you at least gave it a shot.

No one does really well at something new. Keep at it and you'll get better.

No matter how often you fail, *you* never become a failure.

Let's recall some concrete evidence that you're *not* stupid.

You can, too, handle frustration. Don't sell yourself short.

Now that you've seen a few examples, you can probably generate more of your own. And now for the best part: Consider how your discouraged friend would begin to feel if he or she truly listened to you. If you think he or she would be less discouraged and more likely to keep trying, you're absolutely right. A substantial body of research has shown that when people change their thinking, their feelings and behaviors follow suit.

But let's not get ahead of ourselves. Changing how you think is the subject of the next chapter. The focus of this chapter is developing skill at paying attention to your thoughts and feelings. To paraphrase an old proverb: If you don't know where you are, how will you know where you're going?

Remember, learning therapy skills is no different from learning tennis or piano or French. You can't develop a skill without *practice*. So when you catch yourself feeling miserable and perhaps thinking about suicide, ask yourself the following questions:

- What **emotion** am I experiencing right now? Sadness? Anger? Hopelessness? Fear?

- What is the **situation** I find myself in right now that is giving me trouble?

- What was I **thinking** about just now that made me feel this way?

The purpose of asking yourself these questions is to educate yourself about your experience, rather than simply suffering helplessly. Eventually, this learning process will point directly to things that you can change. The evolutionary purpose of pain is to instruct the sufferer as to what is wrong and what needs to be done to relieve the pain. You can use your emotional pain and suicidal impulses in the same way.

Form for Monitoring Thoughts and Feelings

Date	Trigger Event	Interpretation (Including suicidal thoughts)	Feelings/ Behaviors	Soothing New Interpretation

On the previous page we have provided a form you can use to monitor your thoughts and feelings and to begin to practice changing your interpretations. For now, focus mainly on just listing thoughts and feelings; if you try to change your interpretations and find it difficult, don't worry. That's covered in the next chapter.

We recommend that you duplicate this form and fill out at least five of them before moving on. You can use present, past, or even imagined trigger events. These events should range from relatively common upsets (such as making a mistake at work) to highly painful experiences (such as being lied to or rejected).

To check whether your identified interpretations are on target, ask yourself, "Does it make sense that someone thinking X would end up feeling and doing Y?" In addition, use a friend or counselor as a sounding board. As we said earlier, most thoughts, beliefs, and interpretations are outside of immediate awareness; so it's normal not to be particularly in touch with them at first. Someone who knows you well and who is willing to treat you with kindness and respect can be tremendously helpful in your quest to "know yourself" better.

Answer Key to Exercise 6[*]

Dangerous Belief	Cognitive Distortion
I'm inadequate and a loser.	labeling, disqualifying the positive
I can't stand the pain.	jumping to conclusions, magnification
I'm so bad, this is what I deserve.	labeling, jumping to conclusions
If I want something very much, then I can't live without it.	shoulds, musts, oughts all-or-nothing thinking
I just can't cope like other people.	jumping to conclusions, disqualifying the positive overgeneralization
Hurting myself is the only way I can get what I need from others.	jumping to conclusions
No one would miss me if I were gone.	jumping to conclusions, disqualifying the positive
They'll be better off without me.	personalization, mental filter
They'll be sorry.	jumping to conclusions
Life's a bitch and then you die.	mental filter, disqualifying the positive
Hurting myself is the only way to feel better.	jumping to conclusions
This life will never give me what I need.	jumping to conclusions
I'll never be loved.	jumping to conclusions
The next life will be better.	jumping to conclusions.
The future holds nothing for me but pain.	mental filter, jumping to conclusion
Self-harm is my best or only solution.	jumping to conclusions mental filter
I have no reason to go on.	mental filter

---

[*] This answer key is subject to interpretation, so do not worry if your answers did not match exactly. Many of the categories of cognitive distortions overlap somewhat. The spirit of the assignment is most important, which encourages you to question your depressive thinking. It may be instructive to discuss this with your therapist.

7

Step Three: Where Goes the Head, the Rest Will Follow: You *Can* Change How You Think (and *Feel*)

This chapter is about feeling better by changing how you think. You probably recognize this as the cornerstone of cognitive therapy. Because it is such an important element in your process of change, this will be the longest chapter in the book. We will cover the T.E.S.T. process of evaluating and changing unproductive thinking; discuss how thoughts, feelings, and behaviors influence one another; present cognitive (mental) strategies for changing suicidal thoughts; and show you how you can change your thinking by changing your behavior. So much information can seem overwhelming, so we recommend that you cover the chapter a little at a time, allowing yourself plenty of time and opportunity to absorb the information and practice the strategies.

T.E.S.T.: A Recipe for Change

Now that you have begun to explore the role that your thinking plays in fueling your suicidal feelings and impulses, what thoughts do you notice yourself having? Pay attention to these, write them down, and notice the effect they have on your mood and behavior right now.

For example, if you are thinking, "Enough talk, already. Just tell me how to change these thoughts that cause me so much trouble!" then the feeling you are having is probably impatience, and you may find yourself paying close attention and reading faster. Good for you! On the other hand, if you're thinking, "Sure I have negative thoughts; so what else is new? Changing is easier said than done. There's no way this can help me," then you are probably feeling discouraged and have an urge to throw this book in the trash and go to bed. If that's the case, we urge you to keep reading anyway. There's a good chance you will find what follows to be simpler than you expect. Practice talking to yourself with reassuring statements such as, "What harm can it do? At least if I read on I'll have the satisfaction of knowing what's there."

Without a doubt, self-change *is* easier said than done. But be careful not to equate that with impossible. When you think about it, almost everything is easier said than done, from baking a cake to landing on the moon. Usually, the difference between being able to "say" something and being able to "do" something is having relevant information and getting some guidance; and that's exactly what's coming up in this chapter.

Changing your thoughts and feelings requires several steps, which can be easily remembered with the acronym T.E.S.T. Although this process has been taught using other acronyms (most notably, Albert Ellis's A-B-C model), we chose this one to emphasize the technique of adopting the attitude of a scientist. Like the scientist, you will make a habit of TESTing attitudes and beliefs for validity, rather than assuming that all of your depressed and suicidal thoughts and feelings must be true and appropriate. Here are the steps:

Take stock of your reactions to an event (your thoughts, feelings, and behaviors).

Evaluate the thoughts and beliefs that were triggered by the event.

Substitute helpful thoughts and beliefs.

Try the new way.

Let's now go into each of these steps in more detail.

T: Take Stock of Your Reactions to an Event (Your Thoughts, Feelings, and Behaviors)

If you read Chapter 6 and practiced the skills, you already know how to take this first step. To repeat an important point from that discussion, you can't know how (or even what) to change unless you are skilled at identifying problem feeling states, behaviors, and the thoughts that are behind them. We recommend you do this, not by abstractly asking yourself, "How do I feel?" but by monitoring your strong reactions to specific events. So, a more productive question would be, "What am I **thinking** in response to what Mom said this morning to cause me to feel despair and want to engage in suicidal **behavior**?"

As also explained in the previous chapter, it is of utmost importance to *write this down.* Trying to do this only between your ears has a way of generating more heat than light, with the result that nothing much changes. So once again, *write, write, write!* You can use the forms you made in Chapter 6, as well as those that appear later in this chapter.

E: Evaluate the Thoughts and Beliefs Triggered by the Event

In Chapter 6, we discussed some of the more common cognitive distortions that account for a great deal of human suffering. Detecting thinking errors is a crucial skill that is learned only through vigilance and practice. Unfortunately, you probably did not learn how to "think about thinking" in school, so the process might feel rather foreign. Therefore, we devote much of this chapter to ways to determine the validity of your thinking. In the Evaluate step, you will learn to challenge your own pain-producing thoughts by asking yourself questions such as the following:

- Is that thought really true, or does it only feel true?

- Where's the evidence for that thought? If there is none, then what belief is suggested by the evidence?

- Where does it get me to talk to myself this way?

- Is there some other way to interpret this event?

- Is this what I'd say to a good friend in similar circumstances?

S: Substitute Helpful Thoughts and Beliefs

You can probably see how the Evaluate step leads naturally into the Substitute portion of the T.E.S.T. process, for questions like these often answer themselves. However, by no means is it always obvious where to go once you have determined that a given thought is illogical or invalid. Therefore, we will devote much of the present chapter to showing you a variety of ways to change dysfunctional thoughts once you have identified them.

T: Try the New Way

This fourth and last step in the T.E.S.T. process may seem obvious, but you would be surprised how often we find that patients learn all of the requisite skills but get disappointing results because they didn't give the "new way" adequate time and effort. For example, if you were to determine that you regularly engaged in "fortune-telling," as reflected in your hopeless view of the future, you would benefit very little unless you made a regular and persistent effort to pay attention to when fortune-telling was occurring and worked actively to challenge it.

In other words, old habits die hard. As much as we might wish otherwise, thinking patterns we have been "practicing" daily for years and years will not go away simply because we have an insight that they are not "logical." We must be willing to be vigilant and willing to respond as if to say, "Oops! There I go again!"

We will come back to this important issue at the end of this chapter. But first, let's look at specific ways to challenge pain-producing thoughts and adopt new, healthy attitudes and beliefs.

How Thoughts, Feelings, and Behaviors Influence One Another

Before we begin looking at specific ways to change thoughts and feelings, it's important first to become familiar with a basic fact about how human beings operate. What we commonly view merely as "living" actually consists of three interacting processes, as shown in Figure 7-1.*

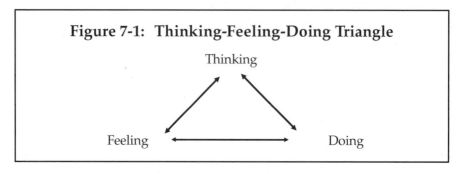

Figure 7-1: Thinking-Feeling-Doing Triangle

Thinking

Feeling   Doing

This model is best explained with an example. Consider "Lisa," a young, divorced nurse, whose boyfriend recently informed her that he was interested in someone else and no longer wished to see her. At the top of the triangle, she might think, "This proves how unlovable I really am. Now I'll never find someone to love!" Such thinking would have a major impact in the Feeling area of the triangle (notably, depression and feelings of hopelessness and inadequacy), as well as in the Doing area (such as crying and giving up on efforts to meet someone new). But the process doesn't stop there, for Feeling and Doing also influence Thinking. In Lisa's case, upon reflecting on her depressed feelings and behaviors, she might think, "See, not only am I unlovable, but I'm also a sad, pathetic creature who gives up when things get tough." This new thought then begins to affect her feelings and behavior, and she is now caught in a vicious, self-perpetuating circle.

Try applying this model to one or two recent experiences of your own. Remember, the model applies not only to vicious circles but to "victorious"

---

* This model has been used by therapists for many years. We did not create it, but have been unable to discover who did.

circles as well; for just as dysfunctional thoughts lead to dysfunctional feelings and behavior, so do functional thoughts lead to functional feelings and behaviors. This helps explain how millions of rejected lovers manage to find the "other fishes in the sea."

Now for the main point of this discussion: *The Thinking-Feeling-Doing triangle is not merely a model of how we experience things; it is also a blueprint for change.* What this means is that change in any area of the model (Thinking, Feeling, or Doing) will likely produce change in the other two areas. Suppose that Lisa, by talking to a friend or counselor or through reading a book such as this one, changed her thinking along the following lines: "Sure, this was a major loss, but it in no way proves that I am unlovable. In fact, I have lots of evidence that I *am* lovable. Now, what can I do to be kind to myself, instead of locking myself in my room?"

What would we expect to be the impact of such a change on Lisa's feelings and behaviors? First, we could expect her feelings to change from depressed, hopeless, and inadequate to sad (she has just suffered a loss, after all) yet hopeful and adequate. Furthermore, we could expect a major change in her behavior, from social withdrawal and isolation to appropriate self-care and nurturing.

Let's now take the model one step further. Suppose Lisa is less than successful at changing her thinking along the lines just described. Can you see how she still has not exhausted her options? For she also can initiate changes in her *behavior* that will benefit her thinking and feelings. For example, Lisa might call a friend or take herself to a movie, thereby disproving her thought, "I always give up when the going gets tough." Change can be initiated through *doing* just as well as (and sometimes better than) through changing thoughts.

Thus, the stage is set for the remainder of this chapter. In the first part of the chapter that follows, we will show you how to feel better by changing your thoughts and feelings through *thinking* processes. Later in the chapter, we will explain how to change your thoughts and feelings by making changes in *behaviors*.

Cognitive Approaches to Changing Suicidal Beliefs

Just as there are many ways to improve physical health—exercising, eating healthy foods, getting plenty of rest, and so on—there are also many "right" ways to acquire healthy thinking habits. In the following sections, we will tell you how to use a variety of methods to change your depressed, suicidal thinking into thinking that will leave you less vulnerable to upset and more aware of what makes life worth living.

Cognitive approaches to healthier (and happier) thinking fall into three general categories: (1) the functional approach, (2) logical/empirical approaches, and (3) questioning approaches. Each category contains one or more specific strategies. Remember, because everybody is different, all approaches may not be equally helpful to all people. However, be sure to try each approach, since that's the only way of knowing whether it will work for you. We encourage you to try each approach lots of times to get the advantage of the practice that might make a strategy more likely to work.

Remember, too, that these strategies assume that you have learned how to identify your feelings and troublesome thoughts. If you don't feel at least moderately confident in your ability to identify your upset-producing thoughts, return to Chapter 6 and allow yourself more practice before moving on.

The Functional Approach: Where's This Getting Me?

The functional approach is perhaps more aptly called the "Where's this getting me?" approach. It is one of the simplest yet most effective strategies. It requires only that you identify your upsetting thought and ask yourself what purpose it serves.

For example, "Frances," an engineering major at a local university, learned through her thought monitoring that one of her most common interpretations whenever she made a mistake was "I'm an idiot." Because she, like all human beings, frequently made mistakes, Frances learned that she was giving herself this label many times a day. At best, when this happened, she felt unhappy with herself; but on bad days, it was only a short step from "I'm an idiot" to "I might as well kill myself."

Let's listen in on a portion of one of Frances's therapy sessions to see how "where's this getting me?" was employed.

Therapist: What purpose does that statement, "I'm an idiot," serve when you say it to yourself after you make a mistake?

Frances: It helps me do better in the future.

Therapist: Can you say more about that?

Frances: Well, if I weren't hard on myself when I screwed up, there's no telling what would become of me.

Therapist: I see. So, how's it working so far?

Frances: What do you mean?

Therapist: What I'm asking is, where's it really getting you to call yourself an idiot whenever you make a mistake?

Frances: Depressed and discouraged, that's what!

Therapist: Has calling yourself names wiped out mistakes in your life?

Frances: No way. If anything, I seem to make more.

Therapist: Can you see what's happening here?

Frances: Yes. I've been thinking I needed to call myself names to motivate myself to do better, when what it really does is make me miserable about my mistakes.

Therapist: Exactly. Now, where do you go from here?

Frances: I'm not really sure.

Therapist: Well, look at it this way: What would you say to your daughter, if she had just made a mistake and you wanted her to learn from the mistake but not be miserable about it?

Frances: I'd tell her that everyone makes mistakes and that mistakes are one of the best ways to learn.

Therapist: Would you call her an idiot?

Frances: Of course not!

Therapist: Now, what does this mean for you?

Frances: I guess I'd better get rid of the name-calling and focus more on how I can learn from my mistakes.

As you can see, the functional approach is relatively simple but powerful. But remember, it won't do you any good if you don't use it. Take a few minutes now, and on a sheet of paper, list your three "favorite" self-critical thoughts. After each one, respond to the question, "Where does that thought get me?" If the answer is "Nowhere" or "Miserable," jot down a few alternative thoughts, more or less along the lines of the therapy session example. As always, give yourself the chance to be a beginner for a while—you'll get better with practice.

Logical/Empirical Approaches: Asking Questions That Put Upsetting Thoughts to the Test

As we have just seen, the functional approach considers the impact of certain thoughts and beliefs on your life. Logical/empirical approaches are different in that they evaluate the actual *validity* of the thought. In other words, in various ways, you ask the question, "Does that make sense?" These methods are in no way incompatible with the functional approach; in fact, you might often find yourself moving from one to the other, seeing the negative impact of a belief (functional approach) to looking at why that belief is illogical or invalid (logical/empirical approach).

Most of us have a common-sense understanding of what the word *logical* means. The word *empirical* is less familiar among nonscientists, but its meaning is straightforward. The word *empirical* refers to anything that is based on *evidence*. Scientists use empiricism, for example, to learn whether a medicine works. In other words, rather than rely on mere *opinions* that the drug is safe and effective, they conduct rigorous experiments that produce evidence regarding the drugs effects.

The justice system also works empirically. A jury's role is to decide, on the basis of hard evidence, whether an individual is guilty of a crime. Imagine if you could be hauled into court, accused of a terrible crime, and convicted based only on the *feelings* of a jury, with no compelling evidence whatsoever. Yet this is what you are doing to yourself every time you call yourself stupid or bad or tell yourself you deserve to die—you are convicting yourself of a crime on the basis of emotion and without valid evidence.

We will examine four logical/empirical methods for challenging depressing and suicidal thinking:

- Demanding evidence

- Collecting data

- Asking better questions

- Putting upsetting thoughts to the test

Demanding Evidence

This method is every bit as simple as it sounds. It means refusing to accept upsetting thoughts, self-accusations, and hopeless predictions of the future without *valid* supporting evidence. Note the emphasis on the word *valid*.

Suppose, for example, that a salesman is trying to sell you an expensive refrigerator, claiming that it is the best on the market. And suppose that when you asked for evidence supporting this claim, he said, "I have no evidence; it's just my opinion." Is this "evidence" valid? Would you fork over your hard-earned money on the basis of such flimsy evidence? Unless you wanted to contribute to the Appliance Salesman Charity Drive, the answer is probably "no."

Now imagine you are a member of a jury considering the guilt or innocence of a man charged with murder, and the prosecutor's entire case is based on the fact that this man was once seen littering. Would you vote to convict and perhaps send the defendant to his death? Of course not; because however wrong this man's previous behavior might have been, it in no way proves he is a murderer. In other words, such evidence would not be considered valid in a court of law.

Now, consider a depressing, potentially suicidal, thought such as, "I'm a complete failure and always will be." Again, we can ask, what is the evidence for such a condemning thought? In some cases, you will quickly see there is no evidence and you will be surprised how immediately you feel better. At other times, the "prosecutor" inside you will respond, "Here's the evidence right here: You've just been fired from your third job." Ouch! At first impact, this might feel like compelling evidence; but is it?

To answer this question, we must go back to our discussion on labeling and overgeneralization. What any scientist and most lawyers will tell you is that this evidence shows *only* that we have a human being who has been fired three times—no more, no less. And pursuing the evidence a little further would show that this human being, far from being a "total failure," has actually succeeded at lots of things in life.

Table 7-1: Where's the Evidence?

Self-Statement	Bogus Evidence	Valid Interpretation
I'm a total failure.	I've been laid off from two jobs.	I do have trouble keeping jobs, but that's only part of me. I have succeeded in other things in life.
I can't stand being alone.	I feel so desperate when I'm alone.	I do prefer to have a mate, but I have "stood" being alone many times. In fact, some of my best times have been when I was on my own.
Nobody cares about me.	The phone hasn't rung in three days.	This only proves no one has called me. There are many people I haven't called lately, and that doesn't mean I don't care about them.
The future holds nothing for me.	Life has been bad for as far back as I can remember.	Although the past can sometimes be used to make predictions about the future, the past doesn't *determine* the future. Experience shows that people change their lives for the better all the time.
Hurting or killing myself is the best solution to my problems.	I can't think of any other solutions.	Appearances can be deceiving. I can discover better solutions by talking with someone who cares.

Table 7-1 presents a few more examples, with answers to the question, "Where's the evidence?" Note that we have listed both invalid (bogus) and valid interpretation. Try a few of your own for practice.

Collecting and Acting on New Data

In addition to examining existing evidence for or against your beliefs, you also can actively gather *new* evidence in various ways. Figure 7-2 shows a four-step process that you can use to challenge bogus evidence for suicidal thoughts (this method can be used to change any troublesome beliefs, but for now we will focus only on suicidal thoughts).

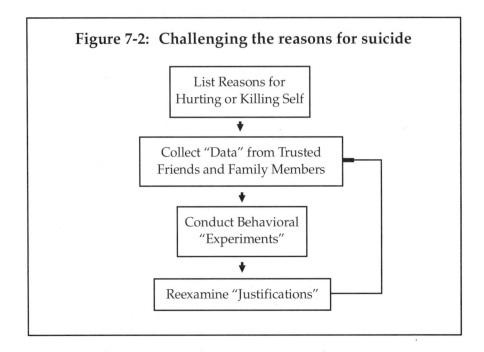

Figure 7-2: Challenging the reasons for suicide

List Reasons for Hurting or Killing Self

Collect "Data" from Trusted Friends and Family Members

Conduct Behavioral "Experiments"

Reexamine "Justifications"

Step one in actively testing your beliefs is to list all of the reasons that occur to you for committing suicide. There's just one catch—the reasons have to be *testable*. What this means is that your reasons need to be stated in such a way that, like a good empiricist, you can see for yourself whether they are valid.

For example, if some of your listed reasons for dying include "The rest of my life will be awful anyway" or "I'll never be able to get over my misery," these do not qualify as testable reasons because no one has a crystal ball. The only way you could truly test these beliefs would be to live out the rest of your life and see what happens. While we are certainly in favor of your living out your natural life, we understand that it is unlikely that very many people would seriously consider waiting around for years or decades just to prove a point or test a theory.

Instead, we recommend an approach that reveals the validity or invalidity of your reasons for wanting to die. Examples of common, testable reasons behind thoughts of suicide include

- Nobody cares about me.

- I'm a complete failure as a person.

- I can't beat my alcohol/drug problem. The only answer is to die.

- I can't live with myself. I hate everything about me and everything I do.

- My life is completely out of control. The only thing I have control over is hurting myself.

Do any of these beliefs ring true to you? They are but a few examples of items that we encounter on our patients "Reasons for Wanting to Die" lists. Such beliefs can be tested in the here and now, or in the near future, thus making our next therapeutic step accessible to people who are in acute emotional pain now. Interestingly, the here-and-now "experiments" (which we will outline shortly) are part of the process by which you will be able to plan for a better future to combat hopelessness and repeated disappointment. This brings us to the next step in challenging bogus evidence.

Step two involves your getting an outside opinion. It is dangerous to make life-and-death decisions based on mere assumptions such as nobody cares about you or you are a complete failure. When you are in the throes of a deep depression, it is impossible to be entirely objective about things like this; and if you isolate yourself, you never allow yourself the opportunity to disprove some of your worst theories about yourself. On the other hand, it can be extremely helpful to talk to people you know in order to get their viewpoints on the matter.

Choose one, two, or maybe three people you know with whom you can sit down and have a frank discussion about how you're feeling about yourself. *Warning: Do not choose people who are highly critical or emotionally abusive.* Instead, choose people who are friendly, likeable, psychologically healthy, and trustworthy—maybe a friend, relative, coworker, mentor, therapist, neighbor, or clergyperson. Tell them how you've been feeling and about your negative views of yourself and your life. (Whether or not you tell them about your thoughts about suicide is entirely up to you—you are under no obligation to divulge this information. However, if you are going to take the step of consulting with trusted others, consider letting them know that you've been wondering if life is worth living. Give them the chance to show their care and concern for you.)

Ask them for their opinions. Do they think that you are a terrible person? Do they think your life is meaningless? Do they see you as a complete failure? Would they agree that people would be better off without you? Talk to more than one person about this, if you can. Listen to what they have to say. If they surprise you with supportive, caring responses, ask them why they feel this way about you. In sum, get a healthy, objective, outside opinion and contrast it with your own subjective, pain-ridden viewpoint. Remember, these are the opinions of people whose judgment you trust. Think about that, and then proceed to the next step.

Step three involves your running small "experiments" to start testing your worst beliefs about yourself and your life. If you feel that your life is out of control, think of things that you can do to reassert control over your actions and activities (we'll discuss some examples in a moment). If you think you are a complete failure as a person and a burden to others, plan to do one or two things that you do well that you may not have done for a while, and arrange to do some nice and helpful things for people you care about.

If you are certain you're a slave to an addiction and that this makes you a "bad" person who cannot change, attend a support-group meeting or look into detoxification treatment at a nearby hospital. If you hate yourself because of things you've done or things that have happened to you that make you feel guilty and ashamed, begin to consider things you can do make amends, if that is possible. Apologize to people you believe you have hurt; unburden your guilt and shame to someone who may be able to put things in a different perspective or who may be willing to return to being on good terms with you. Begin to do things that instill a sense of pride in yourself again, and give yourself a daily goal that will help you to gain a sense of accomplishment and purpose.

An example of someone who used this process to feel better is "Jerry," who was considering suicide because, as he said, "I can't live with myself anymore." He was tired of "screwing up," meaning that he continued to go back to abusing drugs and alcohol even after he had repeatedly promised his family that he would remain clean and sober. He believed that he was nothing but a burden to his loved ones, that he had destroyed his credibility, that he would be plagued by legal and employment problems for the rest of his life, and that he would be rendered helpless by his isolation from others and by his ongoing cravings for substances.

Jerry's therapist helped him work out the following plan to actively address his shame and his sense that he was a burden: (1) Stop making promises for now, (2) stop making excuses, (3) deal with criticism from his family without becoming defensive or seeking solace in alcohol and drugs, (4) start looking for a job, (5) go to Alcoholics Anonymous or Narcotics Anonymous at least five times a week, (6) begin to engage in some of the hobbies and recreational activities he used to enjoy and take pride in doing (for example, billiards, bowling), and (7) send as much money as he could manage to his estranged wife and their two children.

Jerry was by no means perfect in following this agreement, but it gave him something concrete and productive to do to start feeling better about himself again. Jerry's problems continued to pose great challenges to him, but he began to feel a gradually increasing sense of mastery and control over his life, and his suicidality faded. These concrete steps were crucial in Jerry's quest to empirically disprove his theory that he was a hopeless failure.

Step four in testing your problem beliefs requires that you reexamine the evidence after you have engaged in the first three steps (listing your reasons for wanting to die, consulting with others in order to get feedback and support, and starting a new plan of action to retake control over your life). It requires that you take stock of some of the more positive, alternative ways of looking at things that people have encouraged you to consider. It also requires that you calmly evaluate how much you have actually begun to do things differently in order to break out of old, depressive, perhaps self-defeating modes of operation.

If your evaluation of your progress at step four leaves you disappointed, that's your cue to return to step two—consult with the same trusted individuals as you did before. Ask them how they think you're doing and whether they have noticed any changes in you. Ask them where they think you have made positive strides, and ask them for further feedback and suggestions on those areas where you have not met with as much success as you would like. Ask them if they still have concerns about you, even if you do not. Healthy, trustworthy others are an incredibly important asset in life. It is therefore vital to nurture your relationships with such people and to communicate with them on a regular basis about how you're feeling and how you're doing with your self-help projects.

Once you've done step two again, recycle through steps three and four so you can continue to make concrete changes toward the goal of taking charge of your life, thus combating the depressive beliefs that you have no control and no hope. Again, don't go through it alone! If you can't consult with a friend or relative, find a support group or a therapist. Positive life changes are accelerated when you connect with others.

Asking Better Questions: NRQs and PLQs

Although we cannot presume to know and understand you as an individual, we think it is safe to make two assumptions about you. The first assumption is that, like all human beings, you have a strong will to live—a "survival instinct," if you will. The mere fact that you are reading this book is solid evidence that, however much it might flicker at times, your will to live endures. It is well known that a survival instinct exists in all animals, and human beings are no exception.

The second assumption is that for you or anyone to have considered suicide, the problems must be overwhelming and the pain very great. Considering that we all are born with a strong survival instinct, it follows that it would take extreme and prolonged suffering for any of us to reach the point where we wanted to die. A person in this state would have to view the suffering as overwhelming, out of control, and destined to continue without remitting. Under these conditions, it becomes more understandable that he or she would consider simply ending it all rather than continuing the fight. But consider the following questions:

- What if it could be shown that your suffering *could* be managed, such that you would not feel so overwhelmed?

- What if you could show yourself that you had *some* degree of control over the source of your suffering, the way you dealt with it, and your choices in responding to it?

- What if you discovered that your pain did not have to be unrelenting; that it could be predictably temporary or at the very worst, intermittent?

The point of these questions is to suggest that, in spite of what you're going through now, there is still hope for you to attain contentment, joy, hope, enthusiasm, and an overall sense that you're okay and the world is okay. To commit suicide is to forfeit the opportunity ever again to experience this. Choosing to live means giving yourself permission to learn how to manage your pain and to heal.

You might have noticed that the questions we just asked are rather different from the kinds of questions you usually ask yourself. If you have been burdened by significant levels of depression and anxiety, you might have the self-defeating habit of asking yourself *negative rhetorical questions (NRQs)*.

A rhetorical question is a question that requires no answer because it answers itself. A negative rhetorical question, or NRQ, is asked in such a way that a negative answer is assumed. Perhaps some of the following examples of NRQs sound familiar to you:

- Why bother even trying?

- Who gives a damn about me anyway?

- What if I never get over this problem?

- How can I possibly ever change?

- Who would even notice if I were gone?

- What if I wind up totally alone?

- What's the point of going on with life?

- Why should I prolong my suffering by living?

We have found that people considering suicide ask themselves harmful, deceptive questions like these all the time. But NRQs serve no constructive purpose. They simply make you feel worse and trick you into seeing your life as a worst-case scenario. The danger is that NRQs are often automatic aspects of thinking that go unnoticed and unchecked; but the damage they do to your emotions and to your spirit are very real and very significant.

In order to be fair to yourself, we recommend that you learn to match your automatic, harmful NRQs with deliberate, truth-uncovering, *positive literal questions (PLQs)*. Unlike NRQs, PLQs do not answer themselves, but rather help search for the truth. For example, if you catch yourself saying, "What's the point of going on with life?" in a dejected, frustrated, hopeless way, try answering the question positively and literally.

Some conversions of NRQs into PLQs follow. Note that converting an NRQ to a PLQ sometimes requires only a change in tone or enunciation. For example:

> *NRQ*: What's the point of going on with life?
> *Presumed answer*: There is none.
> *PLQ*: Okay, so what is the point of going on with life?
> *Possible answers:* The point of going on with my life is to give myself a chance to get more out of life than I'm getting now. The point of going on is to *change* my life, not to *end* it. The point of going on is to show myself that I'm a survivor, and that I can find a way to overcome adversity. The point of going on is to keep trying to accomplish some of the important things I want to accomplish in my life, and not abandon my goals and dreams forever.
>
> The point of going on is to come to accept and even like myself, to let those I care about know that I love them, and to reach out to those people. The point of going on is to reach a new day and, step by step, to get closer to the time when I will be able to smile and laugh again. The point of going on is to be able to look back someday at this time in my life, to talk about it like an old war story, to use my experiences as inspiration for someone else who might be considering suicide and needs my under- standing and support, and to realize that I've made it, I've survived. That's the point of going on!

In summary, the answer to reducing the severity and duration of your emotional reactions is not easy, but it is simple: You must make some basic changes in the ways you think and act, and this will change how you feel. This will not happen overnight. However, if you are willing to commit to life long enough to give this a fair chance, if you are willing to take things a step at a time, if you are willing to practice new ways, and if you are willing to accept that even positive change feels a little strange at first, you will be able to reduce your pain and increase your hope, *regardless of whatever else is going on in your life that may truly be outside of your control*.

If this sounds overly optimistic, ask yourself the PLQ, "What do I have to lose by trying?" If it seems difficult or not worth the effort, ask yourself the PLQ, "How can I make this effort worth my while?" If you're tempted to ask yourself the NRQ, "What if I try everything this book tells me to do but I still don't get it and I'm still suicidal?" respond immediately and resoundingly with the PLQ, "What if I try and I find that I'm starting to feel better and to change my life in a positive way?"

We hope that ultimately you will learn to eliminate most NRQs from your daily automatic thinking. But since that takes time and persistence, the best approach in the meantime is to let no NRQ pass without challenging it with a corresponding PLQ. This is not wishful thinking, sticking your head in the sand, denying your problems, or minimizing how badly you feel. It is refusing to ask yourself loaded questions and, instead, being fair and even-handed with yourself.

Your negative views of yourself, your life, and your future have been promoted for far too long, while your positive views about yourself, your life, and your future have been discriminated against, disenfranchised, and disempowered. It is time to give your optimism and self-care a little affirmative action. It is high time to give all of your thoughts—both positive and negative—a level playing field on which to compete.

Socratic Method: Finding Truth by Asking the Right Questions

Socrates, the fabled Greek philosopher, created a revolutionary new approach to both logic and teaching. Because he believed that the source of truth resided within each individual rather than somewhere "out there," he taught students primarily by asking them questions. The same method can be applied to help you acquire the knowledge you need to feel better. In this section, we will provide you with a few crucial, Socratic questions (PLQs, actually) and show you how to address them in a way that promotes growth and well-being.

To give this method a fair chance to work, it is essential that you sit down and write. If you simply mull over these questions in your head, you are likely to encounter the same problems that have plagued your mood all along—you'll become overwhelmed, lose track of the points you're trying to make, feel like giving up, and wind up with nothing you can get a handle on. So, once again, write, write, write!

Here is the sequence of key questions to ask yourself:

1. What are my reasons for hurting or killing myself, and why do they seem justified?

2. What would I tell a close friend in the same circumstances?

3. How else could I reasonably view my situation?

4. What steps can I take to change my life rather than end it?

5. Why do I sometimes not mind living?

6. How might my life be better in the future?

Key Question 1: What Are My Reasons for Hurting or Killing Myself, and Why Do They Seem Justified?

To address the first key question, list all of the reasons you can think of for killing yourself. For each item you put on your list, add the following sentence: "This seems like a reasonable justification for hurting myself because . . ." and then finish the sentence.

At first, this might seem like the worst possible thing to do. After all, why should you make a case for hurting yourself? The answer is that not to be aware of your reasons for self-harm or self-destruction is actually more dangerous than to spell out your reasons and evaluate them. If you don't come to grips with the fundamental reasons why you think dying is your best option, you won't give yourself a good chance to think things through carefully and possibly uncover critical flaws in your rationale. Instead, you'll remain on emotional autopilot, which can be extremely hazardous when you are deeply distressed.

Detailed here are sample replies to the first key question, written by "Mary," a young patient with depression. Remember, its up to you to think of your own answers to all of these questions—these examples are provided merely to help get you started on your own list.

Mary's Answers to Key Question 1: What Are My Reasons for Hurting or Killing Myself?

1. I should die or hurt myself because *life means nothing without someone who loves you, and I'll never get that.*

This seems like a reasonable justification because *I can't bear to be alone, and I know that I'll end up that way no matter what I do.*

2. I should die or hurt myself because *nobody really loves me—how could they? I don't feel like I'm worthy of someone's love.*

This seems like a reasonable justification to die because *even if someone thinks he loves me, he'll soon realize that I'm unworthy, and then I'll be abandoned, which is even worse than having nobody in the first place.*

3. I should die or hurt myself because *the only thing that was ever half decent about me was my looks, and now I'm getting older and I'll lose my one asset. Nobody can avoid getting older, so my future will be even worse than now.*

This seems like a reasonable justification to die because *my best days are behind me, and everything will just get worse and worse as time goes on.*

Now that she has listed her reasons for harming herself, Mary can take a long, rational look at her own views on life, death, and her worth as a person. She can think things through in a way that she couldn't if she merely kept all of this information vaguely stored in the back of her mind. Now let's move on to the next question.

Key Question 2: What Would I Tell a Close Friend in the Same Circumstances?

This is a powerfully therapeutic question because it almost always stimulates compassion and hopefulness. Depressed individuals often have a much greater capacity to offer consolation, support, acceptance, and constructive advice to the people they care about than they do to themselves. This question brings this unfortunate double standard out into the open for discussion.

Why might this double standard exist? Some people have not learned that it is okay to nurture themselves. Others have learned that it is important to be kind and compassionate to others but that they themselves are not worthy of such kindness. You might like and think highly of a friend and forgive that friend many of his or her human shortcomings without so much as a second thought. But you might see similar shortcomings in yourself and interpret that as justification for self-harm because you are undeserving of anything better.

If you have friends that you like and admire, consider the following important fact. Many studies in the field of social psychology have indicated that one of the main reasons people become friends is that they view themselves as being similar to each other in important ways (interests, personality, life situation, ways of thinking, etc.). Therefore, the people you think of as friends—the people you admire—are probably not much different from you. So it makes sense to allow yourself the same degree of tolerance and compassion that you allow your friends.

Mary's Response to Key Question 2: What Would I Tell a Close Friend in the Same Circumstances?

I would tell her that she is not alone, that there are people who care about her, and that anybody who would leave her because she didn't look her best didn't have the maturity to be a suitable mate anyway. I would tell her that she is lovable—that she's been loved before and she'll be loved again. I would also remind her that she might be lonely at times but that this is not to be confused with being lonely for eternity.

Also, to be without a man is not the same as being unlovable. Finding a love partner is difficult to do, no matter how worthy you are; but it's a little more doable if you can like and accept yourself for starters. I would tell her that her best days are not behind her. In fact, many of her suicidal days are better left behind her. I'd tell her that there are many reasons to feel lovable and to continue living. I'd tell her that I care about her very much and don't want to lose her. That's what I'd tell my friend if she were in my situation and wanted to die.

Key Question 3: How Else Could I Reasonably View My Situation?

The adage "The grass is always greener on the other side of the fence" often comes into play when suicidal individuals take stock of their lives. It is common for such people to be utterly convinced that there is nothing to live for, no redeeming quality to their lives, and no sources of happiness, which they assume other people have. Interestingly, when such people try to end their own lives, they often astound others around them, who think, "How could he try to kill himself? He's such a good, decent person," or "What could make such a lovely woman try to kill herself?" or "It's so difficult to understand. He's got so much going for him. Doesn't he realize that? What state of mind must he have been in to do something so drastic?"

This brings to mind the subject of E. A. Robinson's poem, "Richard Cory," who was viewed by all as so successful, gentlemanly, and handsome, and as possessing the sort of graces that would earn him the envy and admiration of all—and who also went home one evening and "put a bullet through his head." This teaches us a vitally important lesson: *It is not possible to fairly and objectively evaluate your own life if you are in great pain.* When you are feeling suicidal, it is virtually certain that you are underestimating the value and the good in your life. You are considering an irreversible act—suicide—based on opinions that may be inaccurate, fleeting, and certainly not held by others.

Before acting on self-destructive impulses, you owe it to yourself to take every step possible to gain a more balanced view of your life. To that end, let us look at Mary's answer to Key Question 3.

Mary's Response to Key Question 3: How Else Could I Reasonably View My Situation?

I may be unsure of my lovability, but this does not mean that I am unlovable. In fact, many people have told me that they care about me—I just have trouble believing them. I guess they wouldn't lie to me, but for some reason I have difficulty being kind to myself. Since I dislike myself so much, I naturally jump to conclusions that people will reject me the moment they see my imperfections. But the reality is that people

I like and whose judgment I trust seem to care about me, even when I'm at a low ebb in terms of my looks and my sociability. Perhaps I could start paying closer attention to what they see in me that I don't. At any rate, it would be premature of me to kill myself based on the assumption that I'll be rejected, when I seem to be the person who's doing the rejecting. I know that I felt unloved and abandoned by my parents, but that doesn't mean that I'll be unloved and abandoned by my friends. Furthermore, I should not abandon myself in my time of need by killing myself. That would be cruel. I need to support myself at times like this.

Key Question 4: What Steps Can I Take to Change My Life Rather than End it?

Helplessness and hopelessness usually dominate the moods and thoughts of someone contemplating suicide. There is a strong pull to believe that life's troubles are insurmountable and overwhelming and that nothing can be done to improve your lot.

For example, "Linda" thought she had made a dreadful mistake in getting married. She regretted her choice of partner and had serious thoughts about escaping through suicide. So great was her distress, she thought that suicide was a logical solution. However, she seemed stunned when her therapist said to her, "It's remarkable that you would be willing to leave life altogether before you would consider leaving this marriage." This was an apparently obvious suggestion; yet Linda had not truly considered it, nor the concrete steps that she could take to pursue this viable, nonlethal, change in her life. Further inquiry revealed that Linda held dysfunctional beliefs about being a bad person for wanting to leave her husband and that everyone would fault her and shun her if she did. So, instead of pursuing the obvious option, she zoomed right to the most drastic (and lethal) option.

This kind of macabre problem solving is common, even in otherwise intelligent, successful people. As an alternative to this dangerous approach, we strongly encourage you to do some heavy-duty problem solving regarding your life's difficulties. Now let's return to Mary's responses to our key questions.

Mary's Answer to Key Question 4: What Steps Can I Take to Change My Life Rather than End It?

First the easy stuff—I'll get a new hairstylist. I got so upset about my last haircut that suicidal thoughts entered my mind, but why should I die because somebody else can't follow instructions? Second, I need to take pride in things in my life other than my appearance, which to a large degree is superficial (except for my smile, which can be genuine and nice, if I let it). I have to ask myself what activities, projects, and learning experiences I have been neglecting out of fear that I would fail, and go ahead and start doing them! I have to stop assuming that people will judge me solely based on how I look, or based on how I feel about myself, which I know from experience is punitive and negative. I have to listen to the affirmative things that others tell me and not dismiss them as "just being nice."

Key Question 5: Why Do I Sometimes Not Mind Living?

Has it ever seemed a little strange to you that the same life that seems downright unbearable during bad times is okay during the good times? It's the same life, so how can your appraisal of it change so much from one day or moment to another?

What you are experiencing is actually a well-known phenomenon known as "state-dependent recall." What this means is that *we tend to remember whatever is consistent with how we are currently feeling:* If we're feeling good, we're likely to remember the good and if we're feeling rotten, we're likely to remember the bad. This tendency can be resisted if you are alert to it, but it can be very dangerous for a suicidal person if he or she doesn't know how to counteract it.

This negative memory bias is quite common in people who have histories of recurrent depression and who tend to become hopeless about the future. Therefore, as therapists, we are especially aware of the importance of helping our clients to think about the times in their lives when they felt more hopeful and content. Despite their impressions to the contrary, such individuals have typically experienced a considerable degree of happiness in their lives; but this is quickly forgotten or dismissed as soon as a wave of depressed mood takes over.

For example, one of our patients suffered from an atypical, rapidly cycling type of depression. One week she'd be enthused about her life, and the next week she'd be utterly convinced that her prior optimism was "sheer delusion." Soon thereafter, she'd be hopeful and cheerful again. Interestingly, while she was in her "up" phase, she rarely referred to her depressions as being unrealistic or "delusional." She viewed her down moods as being very much a part of herself and her reality. By contrast, when she felt depressed and suicidal, she completely mocked her tendency to feel good and responded to the therapist's expressed support and hope with cynical scorn. Obviously, there was a fundamental bias in her thinking that put her at risk for hopelessness and suicide, even though there was ample evidence that her life was indeed punctuated by meaningful and joyous intervals.

This teaches us that we must take advantage of and pay close attention to the times—or even moments—when we feel good about life and ask ourselves about the realities on which positive moods are based. One way to do this is to answer Key Question 5 in detail. Let's look at how Mary responded:

Mary's Response to Key Question 5: Why Do I Sometimes Not Mind Living?

Sometimes, when I'm not dwelling on what I dislike about myself and when I'm not focusing on my disappointments and regrets, I notice that there are moments when it's okay to be alive. I notice this when I talk to my sister, who has been my best friend all my life and whose little boys I love as if they were my own. I notice this when I listen to music that I like and when I read an interesting book. It feels okay to be alive when the weather is nice and I'm taking a walk, and when I'm taking a drive on an open road. I feel hopeful about being alive when I think about things I might let myself look forward to doing in the future and when I use my imagination to think of interesting things to do, instead of just vegging out at home. Sometimes all it takes is someone saying "thank you" or "I really appreciate your help" or "that was a really good idea" to me, and I allow myself to hear it and believe it. Life hasn't been terribly kind to me the last few years, but I haven't exactly been kind to myself either. If I can start to be nicer toward myself, maybe I'll start a new trend, and then I really won't mind being alive.

Key Question 6: How Might My Life Be Better in the Future?

It is probably safe to assume that by the time a person has decided to commit suicide, she or he has concluded that things will never get better in life. This makes sense; for if someone believed otherwise—that the worst might soon be over—it is unimaginable that he or she would still choose to "check out" of life. The suicidal person almost always is convinced that there is nothing in the future worth waiting around for on planet Earth. The future seems bleak, and that is that.

At the risk of offending readers who believe in prophecy, destiny, or fortune-telling, we must say that *to feel certain about the future always reflects erroneous thinking.* People can make tentative predictions and educated guesses; but we, as mortals, can never be 100 percent accurate in our predictions about what will unfold in our lives.

Suicide, in many respects, reflects an implied belief that you can predict the future with high accuracy. The belief can be summed up this way: "I have seen the future. It holds nothing but misery for me. Therefore, I will cut my losses now by taking my own life." Ironically, the only way to guarantee that the future will hold no promise is to kill yourself, thus ending your chances to find happiness and meaning once and for all. This is a classic case of the "self-fulfilling prophecy."

If you are convinced that the future holds only emptiness and pain, you should think this through carefully. You have nothing to lose by imagining what appealing possibilities life might hold. To paraphrase an old saying, you have to have a dream in order to make your dream come true. What harm can come from allowing yourself to dream a little? Try suspending your belief that things will never change, just long enough to think seriously about how things could be different and what you could do to make it happen. This sets the stage for answering Key Question 6. Let's see what Mary said.

Marys Response to Key Question 6: How Might My Life be Better in the Future?

This is hard. I don't usually allow myself to think about things like this. I am afraid of getting my hopes up. But then, what do I have to lose? I am already considering losing my life, so the least I can do is consider what I might be forfeiting before I go ahead and do it. I guess even though I often feel certain I will wind up alone, the fact is that I do have significant others in my life, and they do seem to care about me. Someday I might get married and have an intimate wedding reception with just our closest friends. We could buy a "fixer-upper" house and work on it together, which would be hard work, but it would feel so good to be in a partnership like that. I could go back to school part-time and finish my degree, which I've always wanted to do but never had the confidence.

I could make a point of keeping in contact with my best friends, who I tend to distance myself from and then feel lonely and guilty. I could do this even if I never get married, because my friends are very important, and I don't have to have a man to survive. I guess if I kept up all my contacts with my friends, they would also try to help me in getting introduced to eligible men.

Also, I really would like to see my nephews grow up. I love them so much, and I think I am their favorite relative besides their parents. I don't want to miss out on seeing their development, and I want always to be there for them if they need my support and advice. I can picture myself ten years from now, doing some of the things I've just mentioned, and saying to myself, "I can't believe I almost ended it all ten years ago. I never would have had any of this. I never believed my life could be happy, but now it's scary to think what I would have given up had I actually killed myself. Thank goodness I changed my mind and had the courage and hope to carry on and keep trying.

Now it's time to practice answering the six key questions yourself. Don't worry if you aren't as articulate as Mary, who happened to be a good writer. Just make an effort to answer in detail and in a self-affirming manner. You'll find you get better as you work at it.

Behavioral Strategies: Changing Self-Destructive Beliefs by Changing What You Do

Lessons from Albert Ellis

As you learned from the Thinking-Feeling-Doing triangle at the beginning of this chapter, it is not always necessary to work at feeling better by changing your thoughts first. In fact, changing behavior can be a very powerful way of changing how you think and feel. In this section, we will show you a process whereby you can *act* so as to change your thoughts and feelings in a therapeutic way.

To understand this process, we turn to Dr. Albert Ellis, founder of Rational-Emotive Therapy:

> Sometimes the best—or indeed the only—way to change a fixed idea is to force yourself to *act* against it: to engage in *live* homework assignments. . . . If you work directly on your feelings, and vividly experience and express them, you may more thoroughly change your crooked thoughts than by directly disputing these irrational Beliefs. . . . In fact, it is doubtful if you ever truly change an irrational Belief until you literally act (and act *many times*) against it (1988, p. 109).

Ellis is fond of telling how, as a young man, he strongly held the belief that to be rejected by a woman was so awful that this risk was to be avoided at all costs. Needless to say, he had very few dates. So he decided to work on this dysfunctional belief by acting against it: For one month, he approached every unaccompanied young woman he saw at a park in New York City—over 100! The outcome? He managed to get only one date, and she stood him up! Nevertheless, his exercise was a resounding success; for through this deliberate effort, he learned that rejection did not kill him, nor did being turned down in any way diminish him as a human being. In fact, he no longer felt the least bit fearful about asking women out. Why? Because by his *actions* he had proven that rejection, while certainly unpleasant, was not the catastrophe that he had imagined it to be.

This is one of many possible examples of how behavioral challenges can be used to eliminate fearful beliefs. But what about beliefs associated with suicidal impulses and behaviors? Consider the belief, "Nothing will ever change; my life will always be miserable." Sound familiar? This thought is behind most suicidal impulses. The problem with it is that, in addition to making you feel bad, it keeps you stuck in the status quo—you are likely to do nothing about the future, because you are convinced that it is useless to try.

Thus, we come to the dreaded *self-fulfilling prophecy:* Because you predict you will fail, you don't try (or you try halfheartedly) to reassert control over your life, which reduces or eliminates any chances that things will get better. As a result, you conclude that you were right all along about the meaninglessness and hopelessness of life and that suicide is a reasonable option.

Notice how this behavior (in this case, not trying) influences thinking (in this case, "proving" that things will never get better). Now, imagine for a moment pursuing a different course of action—acting in a deliberate, proactive way to disprove this belief. You might choose to act in some small way (say, by tidying up your home) or in a big way (such as changing jobs). The point is that you don't have to settle helplessly for what your beliefs are telling you; you can actually *attack* hurtful beliefs by acting against them.

Another idea often seen in suicidal thinking is the belief, "I can't stand it any longer." Are you among the many people who suffer from what Albert Ellis has called "I-can't-stand-it"-itis? If you find those words consistently arising in your internal dialogue, you can attack this desperation-producing belief by intentionally doing things to prove you *can* "stand" things. Start with mild challenges like picking the longest line at the grocery store or intentionally driving at rush hour. You can then work your way up to more significant challenges, including those that occur naturally in your life. If you think you "can't stand" to hear your dad tell that war story one more time, *ask* him about it. If you think you can't stand anyone's disapproval, dial random telephone numbers and ask for Phillipe.

What's to be gained from all of this frustration? Certainly, the purpose is not to create suffering for yourself, but to rid yourself of the false belief that you can't stand things that you definitely can stand. Why is this important? Because "I can't stand it" is an extremely dangerous idea for a person who has suicidal thoughts. One has to wonder, how many suicide victims would still be around today if, during that last, trying life experience, they had been more aware of the truth: "I don't like it, but I most certainly *can* stand it!"

Here are a few more dysfunctional beliefs to give you practice creating behavioral challenges. For each belief, see how many things you could do to disprove the belief. Don't hesitate to involve your therapist or trusted friends and family members in this exercise.

- I have to be perfect.
- I can't do anything when I'm depressed.
- I have to drink when I feel this way.
- Cutting myself is the only way to feel better.
- I'm a bad person.
- I can't stand being alone.

There is an old saying out in the tradition of Alcoholics Anonymous: "If you keep doing what you're doing, you'll keep getting what you've got." In other words, you must start *doing things differently* in order to reap the benefits of a better life.

Important Pointers

Before concluding this chapter, consider a couple of pointers that will help you succeed at whatever strategies you select out of the many we have described.

Staying Aware and Practicing Moment to Moment

Believe it or not, the greatest challenge in implementing these or any self-change strategies is not learning the terminology or techniques, but *staying mindful* of the therapeutic agenda throughout the hours, days, and weeks of your life. As you know, life has a way of tossing up certain distractions from time to time; things like demanding bosses, unreasonable parents or children, flat tires, toothaches, and the like.

Ironically, times when it is toughest to pay attention to our feelings, thoughts, and behaviors are the very times when we need to the most. Stressful events are highly effective at triggering dysfunctional thoughts that lead to major upset, and it is crucial to plan ways to implement your self-help strategies in the midst of such events. Here are some suggestions:

- Anticipate stressful events whenever possible and rehearse how you can talk to yourself in a helpful rather than harmful manner.

- Write helpful reminders from this book and other sources on index cards and carry them with you for times when upset is clouding your thinking.

- Place "sticky notes" on mirrors or other conspicuous places to remind you of whatever issue you are currently working on.

- Arrange a regular time for yourself (at least 20 minutes three times a week) for self-therapy sessions focusing on your priorities for change.

- Keep a diary documenting progress in areas of importance to you, and refer to it whenever you feel as if you aren't getting anywhere.

- Plan on spending *the rest of your life, if necessary*, working on your happiness. Remember, just because your teeth are clean doesn't mean you can quit brushing your teeth. Emotional well-being is no different—it, too, requires continual attention and care.

If at First You Don't Succeed . . .
Remember the Second "T"

Let us now return to the T.E.S.T. model for another important re-minder: Don't forget the second "T." In other words, "Try" is a critical con-cluding step in the process of recognizing and changing dysfunctional thinking. While it is important not to discourage yourself by overestimating the difficulty of self-change, it would also be self-defeating to mistakenly think it should happen overnight with little or no effort.

We say this in the same spirit we would encourage new skiers or tennis players not to give up if they don't get the hang of it the first day out; to do so would be to risk unnecessarily missing out on a lifetime source of enjoy-ment. Of course, the stakes in this book are much higher than in any mere sport, because we are talking about your life itself. This all is the more reason to be persistent in your efforts to make changes. As simple as some of these strategies may seem, no one gets them overnight. So don't think it's just you. As with most things that are truly worthwhile, hard work and persistence are necessary if you are to reap the benefits. And the benefits can be expected to be well worth the effort.

Summary

Because of the length of Chapter 7, we include a summary of its most impor-tant points. If any of these are still unclear to you, we recommend that you go back and review these sections before moving on to Chapter 8.

- The T.E.S.T. model provides a step-by-step way to feel better by identifying and changing dysfunctional thinking.

- The Thinking-Feeling-Doing triangle shows the influence of these three aspects of experience on one another.

- There are two routes to changing dysfunctional thoughts: cognitive and behavioral.

- There are three types of cognitive strategies: functional ("Where's this getting me?") logical/empirical ("Where's the evidence?") and socratic questioning ("How else can I view this?").

- Thoughts and feelings also can be changed by *acting* against dys-functional beliefs.

- It is important to stay aware of self-help priorities moment to mo-ment and to be persistent in the process of self-change.

8

Step Four: Feeling Better through Coping (Sometimes Accommodation Is Okay)

In Chapter 3, we presented the A-B-C model of emotional disturbance. As you saw in the previous chapter, changing the B (what you believe and how you talk to yourself about events) is a powerful means of helping yourself feel better. However, by no means is changing your beliefs the only way to defeat upset and suicidal impulses. Just as there are three components to understanding human emotion and behavior (Activating events, Beliefs, and emotional and behavioral Consequences), so too are there three areas in which you can make changes to feel better. These are listed in Table 8-1.

To illustrate, let's imagine that you've just had a particularly unpleasant phone conversation with an important person in your life, such as your mother. As time passes, you become more and more upset as you realize that you never seem quite "good enough" for her. You begin to wonder whether you are even "good enough" to go on living. What are your options in each of these three categories for feeling better?

Change the A: You could attempt to change the situation that is making your life difficult by asking your mother to cut down on the criticism. Failing this, you could reduce or eliminate phone conversations with her.

Change the B: Instead of trying to get rid of your "mom stressors," you could work on changing the way you interpret her behavior by reminding yourself that you don't need your mother's approval to be an okay person and that her critical attitude may be more a sign of her problems than yours.

Change the C: Finally, you have the option of leaving both the situation and your belief system alone and simply practicing good stress management and emotion regulation. To deal with this episode of upset, you could call someone you know who accepts you; meditate; listen to soothing music while soaking in the tub; or get out of the house to do things you enjoy.

This chapter is about "changing the C," an option sometimes referred to as *accommodation*. When you accommodate, you help yourself feel better without making any major, lasting changes in yourself or the situation. We generally advise that it is preferable to make changes at A and B rather than C, because palliative remedies like listening to music or pounding a pillow tend to be only temporary "fixes." You also should know that in some circumstances (such as anytime you are being physically or emotionally abused) accommodation can be a downright bad idea. However, when used wisely, accommodation is a valuable part of anyone's coping repertoire.

We will discuss four kinds of coping: obtaining support, distraction, relaxation, and recreation.

Table 8-1: The A-B-Cs of Change

	A (The situation)	B (What you're thinking about the situation)	C (How you react)
Change strategies	Change the situation	Change how you interpret the situation	Cope with your reaction (accommodation)
Examples of change strategies	Ask others to change their behavior	Learn more effective self-talk	Take extra good care of yourself when upset
	Change jobs	Detect and change thinking errors	Learn effective stress management skills
	Meet new friends	Detect and change irrational beliefs	Contact supportive others to share your feelings
	Learn better problem-solving skills		Practice self-soothing

Obtaining Support

Few things feel better than getting support from someone who is "on our side," yet this is sometimes near the bottom of the list of things we think of when we're upset. Compared to therapy, which generally seeks to change things at A or B, support is aimed mainly at helping people feel that they are not alone in their struggle. In my (TE) work with patients hospitalized in an acute care psychiatric unit, by far the most common response to the question, "What helped?" has been, "Knowing that I'm not alone and that I'm not the only one who feels this way."

In addition to this feeling of shared experience, support can make *brainstorming* possible. This form of problem solving is impossible when you keep everything inside. In one type of brainstorming, two or more people generate possible solutions to problems off the top of their heads without regard to how impractical or unrealistic those solutions may seem. Later, they examine each idea for its respective pros and cons. This process usually results in the generation of ideas that never would have occurred to one person working in isolation, because an idea from one person often triggers one or more ideas in another person. This supports the adage that "two heads are better than one."

You can obtain support in many ways and from many different sources. However, it often is not forthcoming unless you *seek it out*. You might call upon a faithful friend—someone who always seems to be there for you. This can also be a good time to contact someone you haven't been in touch with for a while. Remember, too, that some sources of support are less than obvious: your priest, minister, or rabbi; your physician; your elderly neighbor; or your hairdresser. And by all means, remember the crisis hotline in your community. This is a source of support that's available around the clock, and you needn't be on the verge of suicide to use it.

When seeking support, it is critical that you remain vigilant for any thoughts that might serve to talk you out of it, such as the following:

I don't want to burden anyone.

He's much too busy to bother talking to me.

She will think I'm weak if I ask her for support.

It probably won't help anyway.

If you notice such thoughts, you must challenge them vigorously. Imagine that someone you cared about wanted to talk to you but assumed you were too busy or would think poorly of him if he sought your support. What would you think or say? You probably would wonder where he got such unusual ideas, and you probably would reassure him in no uncertain terms that this is what friends are for. What good is a friendship, after all, if not for support in times of trouble?

It might help allay your concerns about "burdening" someone else to know that when people help others they help themselves as well. The entire self-help movement is based largely on this principle. From Alcoholics Anonymous meetings to suicide hotlines, people who invest in helping others report that they gain a great sense of fulfillment from knowing that their efforts have benefitted someone. Moreover, when you tell others about your troubles, you will be amazed at how often they tell you that they have felt the same way or had similar experiences. As a result, both parties benefit. Obtaining support from others is clearly much more than just finding a shoulder to cry on.

Ventilation

Human emotions are often compared to a teakettle: When they are heated up, pressure begins to build, and letting off steam serves to prevent a possible explosion. Ventilating emotions (known in therapy circles as *catharsis*) can be helpful, but it is important to understand that human beings are considerably more complex than kitchenware.

First, be aware that there are helpful and unhelpful ways to ventilate feelings (the ventilation analogy is generally used in relation to anger, but it can be applied to sadness or anxiety as well). Yelling at a spouse or boss is almost never helpful, because the other person almost always takes offense and finds it necessary to retaliate. This can result in more harm being done than good. However, writing a heartfelt, even irrational, diatribe in red ink and then tearing the paper into tiny pieces can provide some release without doing any particular harm. It can also provide the benefit of some time to cool down and think about the wisest way to approach the situation.

Second, you need to know that in some cases ventilation can make you feel worse. It is a common misconception, for example, that the best way to deal with anger is to "get it out" by screaming in your car or pounding on a pillow until feathers fly. However, as Carol Tavris points out in her important book, *Anger: The Misunderstood Emotion*, ventilation is often only a way to shoot ourselves in the foot. Scientific studies have shown that, contrary to what common sense might tell us, ventilation does not function as a reliable anger reducer. In fact, it often has the *opposite* effect, causing the angry individual to feel even more self-righteous and victimized.

All of this is not to say that ventilation is always a bad idea. Most of us have had the experience of feeling better after a good cry. Similarly, screaming into a pillow (or better yet, having a good laugh) can serve a valuable tension-reducing purpose. What's important is that you pay attention to what works for you. If you don't feel better after crying, this probably shouldn't be part of your standard coping repertoire. If pouring your feelings out on paper helps, you might want to look into buying paper in bulk as a worthwhile investment. Just be sure that you make ventilation an informed choice rather than an automatic reaction to upset. If it doesn't seem to work for you, then you might want to look into some other coping options, some of which are described next.

Using Distraction to Your Advantage

Question: What do television programs, computer games, sunsets, "getting busy," shopping, and football games all have in common? Answer: They all serve as highly effective distractions to divert the attention of millions of Americans from problems and stressors of daily living.

Considering how much time, money, and energy people invest in seemingly meaningless pursuits, it is easy to conclude that these are a bunch of foolish time-wasters. But consider what the typical citizen has to deal with on any given day: news reports about the growing danger of terrorism; environmental catastrophies waiting to happen, from nuclear waste to holes in the ozone layer; AIDS; flat tires; crying babies; water in the basement; corporate downsizing; the rising cost of living. The list goes on and on. It makes sense, then, that healthy people (who want to stay healthy) find ways to distract themselves temporarily from the pressing demands life makes on them. Realizing, of course, that problems will need to be addressed sooner or later, it can make a great deal of sense to take occasional, temporary refuge from the storm.

Indeed, this is one of those places in life where the rule of the golden mean (taking the desirable middle ground between any two extremes) carries much weight. We know all too well the metaphor of the ostrich with its head in the sand. Using distraction as a habitual problem-solving style (for example, playing computer games when you really need to be discussing a problem with the boss) is likely to lead to even greater problems. But by the same token, *never* using distraction to cut yourself a little slack during stressful times can wear you down to the point where you're hardly fit to solve any problems at all.

Think for a moment about a past emotional upset you've experienced, perhaps a suicidal crisis. Would it have been helpful to employ a little healthy distraction as a way to let things cool down? What activities might have helped? Here are a few distractions our patients have shared with us over the years:

Getting busy with housework

Renting a video and making popcorn

Listening to music turned up loud

Going shopping

Playing games at the video arcade

Baking

Going to church

Making dinner for yourself and a friend

Serving meals at a local soup kitchen

Working in the garden

Reading an engrossing novel

Taking a nap

Going bowling

Taking a drive in the country

Doing something you've been putting off

Of course, this list is potentially endless and depends on your own circumstances and preferences. But, be aware that not just any activity constitutes an effective distraction. Remember that the focus here is what you can do for yourself in the midst of significant, potentially suicidal, upset. To be an effective distractor, an activity should have the following characteristics:

1. It should be enjoyable.

2. It should evoke emotions contrary to your upset (for example, if you're feeling angry, don't listen to heavy metal music or watch a movie like *Natural Born Killers*).

3. It should be highly involving (rearranging your sock drawer is not likely to draw your attention away from a major life upset).

4. In most instances, it should involve other people.

5. It should be free of negative long-term consequences.

The last of these is especially important. No matter how effective a distractor is in the short run, the purpose is defeated if you end up paying a price in the long run. Examples of such distractions include getting drunk or high on drugs, going on a shopping spree you can't afford, engaging in impulsive, unsafe sex, and taking excessive risks (such as driving dangerously). Temporary relief is rarely worth such high-stakes risks, especially when alternatives are available without such negative side effects.

We suggest that you make a list right now of your distractors, both the ones you currently use and ones that might be possible for you. Then rate each according to each of the criteria above (you might use a rating scale from 1, meaning the distractor matches the criterion poorly, to 5, meaning it matches very well). This will be an opportunity to cross off activities that are counterproductive and perhaps add new ones that can have life-enhancing effects.

Relaxation: Easier Said than Done

In the 1950s, a pioneering behavioral researcher, Joseph Wolpe (1982), turned an apparently obvious observation into one of the pillars of behavior therapy. The observation was that it is impossible to be both anxious and relaxed at the same time. As a result, relaxation training has become a staple in the therapeutic repertoire of most therapists.

At first glance, many people consider relaxation training about as necessary as lessons in breathing. After all, if you want to relax, all you need to do is sit down and put your feet up, right? Wrong. Although it might be argued that we all are born with the ability to relax, it is clear that many adults have lost this skill somewhere along the way. Many of our patients (and many nonpatients!) tell us that they are unable to relax even when they try. The good news is that, although relaxation is a complex skill, it most certainly can be learned; and it is a skill that improves with practice.

There are many roads to relaxation, and studies have not shown any single method to be superior to the others. Just as there are many ways to get physically fit (aerobics, tennis, weight lifting, jogging, etc.), you also can choose from a variety of relaxation methods to see what works best for you. We will give you a sampling of three basic types of relaxation methods: progressive muscle relaxation, imagery, and mindfulness meditation. Please realize that most people will need more than just an overview to be able to use a technique effectively. Therefore, at the end of each section we will provide recommended reading for further study.

Progressive Muscle Relaxation

Have you ever noticed, during the course of an ordinary day, that your body was doing something you hadn't realized it was doing? Perhaps you became aware that your foot was shaking furiously as you sat through a lecture. Or your jaw was clenched and your hand balled into a fist as you were watching the news on TV. Or your stomach was tense and your knuckles were white as you gripped the steering wheel in the midst of a traffic jam. Or your head, neck, and shoulders suddenly began to ache after a stressful day.

What all of these experiences have in common is the tightening of muscle groups outside of your awareness. Is your body out of control? Not really, for these are all voluntary muscles. But just as you are sometimes unaware of certain thoughts, feelings, and behaviors, so too, can you lose touch with what your muscles are doing. You need to reopen communication channels between your conscious mind and your muscles, and this is the purpose of *progressive muscle relaxation* (PMR).

What follows is a brief sampling of PMR. Since it is impractical to try to read this while doing the exercise, you might read the following passage (slowly) into a tape recorder and play it back during the exercise. Before starting the exercise, be sure to disconnect the phone and take other precautions against being interrupted.

> Begin by making yourself comfortable on a chair or bed, and
> loosen any clothing that may be too tight. Close your eyes and
> remind yourself that this is a special time set aside to take care of

your health, and you are not to be rushed. Take a deep breath and hold it for a moment, noticing the tension you feel in your chest and abdomen. Now slowly allow the air to escape and your breathing to return to normal. Notice the contrast between the states of tension and relaxation. The goal is to move your entire body from a state of tension to a state of relaxation. Take another deep breath, hold it, and let it go. Now spend a few moments just paying attention to your breath, without attempting to change it.

Next, begin to scan your entire body for muscle tension, one muscle group at a time, from the top of your head to the tips of your toes. With each muscle group, you may wish to tighten or flex the muscle in order to increase your awareness of its location. Begin with the muscles in your scalp and forehead. Raise and lower your eyebrows, and again, notice the difference between the states of tension and relaxation. Next, shift your attention to your jaw muscles, a common focus of stress and tension. You may wish to open and close your mouth as a way of loosening this large and powerful muscle group. Focus next on your neck muscles, turning your head from side to side and rolling your head around to release any tension you find there. Now bring your shoulders into awareness. You can shrug your shoulders and fold them forward and backward to help them relax. Allow them to sag just a bit as they become more relaxed. Next, let your attention travel slowly down your arms and into your hands. Tense your hands and arms to raise your awareness of these muscles. Then allow your hands and arms to rest heavily in your lap or on the bed, and notice that with the passage of time they become even more relaxed.

Now focus on your stomach muscles. Permit your stomach to become soft and comfortable, and notice how it rises and falls with your breath. Take all the time you wish just to attend to your breathing. Next, continue your body scan by directing your attention slowly down the length of your legs and into your feet. If you notice any tension in these muscles, allow it to fade away. Imagine that your legs become pleasantly heavy as they become more and more relaxed.

Allow yourself at least another five minutes to experience this increased level of relaxation. Periodically review muscle areas that have been trouble spots, and if you notice tension there, let it go. Afterwards, return your attention to your breathing. If you begin to notice any frustration because you are not as relaxed as you would like, remind yourself that you are just starting out and that your muscles will need time and practice to learn how to relax again. When you are ready to conclude the exercise, remind yourself that you can carry part of this relaxed feeling with you for the remainder of the day, and slowly open your eyes.

To learn more: *The Relaxation Response,* by Herbert Benson (Avon Press); *The Relaxation and Stress Reduction Workbook,* by Martha Davis, Elizabeth Eshelman, and Matthew McKay (New Harbinger Publications).

Imagery

If you have a good imagination, you might be able to put it to work to help yourself cope. You can use imagery techniques alone or with progressive muscle relaxation both to distract you from current life stressors and to induce physical relaxation. As with PMR, set aside a block of time and arrange not to be interrupted. Then take some time to select a mental image of a relaxing and tranquil scene. This might be a time in the past when you felt especially safe and at peace with the world, whether on vacation or snugly in bed on a cold winter's night. Or you can, if you wish, create a scene to your own specifications, as if you were a movie director.

As you picture your scene, strive for the greatest degree of detail possible: Who else (if anyone) is present? How many objects can you picture clearly? What color are they? What's the weather like? See how many senses you can employ in addition to the visual. If you're at the beach, can you feel the warm sun on your skin? Smell the salt air? Hear the waves rolling in? Remember, how you use imagery is limited only by your creativity. For example, you might begin an image by imagining yourself lying on an air mattress on a quiet lake but then change the air mattress into a cloud as you float comfortably, feeling lighter than air. You can even use the exercise to visualize yourself at some future time, coping successfully with whatever life sends your way. As with PMR, you can expect your skill at imagery to increase with practice.

To learn more: *In the Mind's Eye: The Power of Imagery for Personal Enrichment,* by Arnold Lazarus (Guilford Press).

Mindfulness Meditation

Although for many Americans meditation conjures up images of mysterious rituals in faraway places or odd and eccentric people chanting, meditation in reality is a fairly simple practice that has gained considerable respect among clinicians and researchers. Mindfulness meditation has been around for thousands of years and is being introduced to many Americans by Dr. Jon Kabat-Zinn of the University of Massachusetts Medical Center. Kabat-Zinn has used Western methods of science to show that this largely Eastern technique can be beneficial to people with chronic pain, stress disorders, panic disorder, and chronic illnesses. He has also used this technique with prison inmates and professional athletes.

As its name implies, the essence of mindfulness meditation is "paying attention." As with the other methods, it requires setting aside some time on a regular basis to practice. Unlike the other methods, the goal of mindfulness meditation is not to become relaxed so much as to become more mindful of what your mind and body are doing. The result often (though not always) is inducement of deep relaxation.

There are many ways to practice mindfulness, not only while meditating but also throughout your day. For example, have you ever noticed that you hardly tasted your food because you were reading, watching TV, and trying to plan your day during breakfast? Mindfully eating breakfast means paying attention to what you are doing *in the moment* and noticing the taste of the cereal, the sound of the flakes crunching, the aroma of the coffee, and so on. The same principles apply to mindfully attending to a conversation with another person.

Mindfulness meditation is simply the formal practice of mindfulness. Although there are many ways to practice, a good place to begin is breathing meditation. Sit comfortably in a chair or on the floor, close your eyes, and begin to follow your breath. You need not change anything—simply notice what is going on with your breathing. As you do this, you will begin to notice several things. For one thing, you will begin to notice thoughts that take you away from the activity of simply noticing your breathing. These thoughts may be about problems, dinner, or how good a "job" you're doing at meditating. Such thoughts are to be regarded simply as one more thing to notice before returning your attention to your breath. Or you may notice certain things about your body, such as tension in your stomach or a tingling in your toe. You may also notice various emotions, from tranquility to impatience, any of which might trigger more thoughts (such as, "This is silly; I need to get busy and *do* something"). Again, recognize these as simply thoughts (not facts), and gently return your attention to your breath. Begin by practicing for only a few minutes, and then gradually expand the time frame to a half hour or more. As always, practice and persistence are key.

To learn more: *Wherever You Go, There You Are,* by Jon Kabat-Zinn (Delacorte Press).

In summary, relaxation methods have several things in common:

1. The common thread is lowering physical (and emotional) arousal while focusing attention.

2. All are likely to feel awkward at first. It is essential to stick with your chosen method, and you are likely to do this only if you give yourself permission to be a beginner.

3. All of these techniques can be used in stressful situations but will be most beneficial if practiced daily (it makes little sense to wait for a fire to practice a fire drill). Your chances of success will be significantly increased if you keep a written record of your practice.

4. Although seemingly simple, these techniques are easier described than done. Most people can learn a little on their own, but as with piano lessons, it helps *a lot* to have a coach.

Pleasure and Recreation:
Now You Have Permission

Sigmund Freud's statement that the secret to good mental health is "love and work" is one of the most famous sayings in the history of psychology. However, it is increasingly being realized that this great thinker left out a significant factor in the mental health equation: play. Whoever said, "All work and no play makes Jack a dull boy" knew this years ago, but researchers are beginning to show that being dull may be the least of Jack's worries. Indeed, not making time to have fun may make Jack (or Jill) sick.

In their recent book, *Healthy Pleasures*, renowned psychologist Robert Ornstein and physician David Sobel show how modern industrialized society has brought with it a work ethic that has left most of us convinced that the only valid use of time is that which is "productive," or results in some product. Have you ever noticed how good you feel after mowing the lawn or cleaning out a closet, but how guilty you begin to feel when you try to relax? Any attempt at taking a few minutes or hours for idle pursuits (notice the negative connotation to the words) is met with thoughts that spoil it for us. Thoughts like, "I'm really wasting time. I should be doing something productive. There's so much I need to do, and I'm sitting here talking (or reading or watching TV, etc.)."

Ornstein and Sobel use scientific evidence to dismantle the idea that time spent in the pursuit of pleasure is time wasted. In fact, the evidence shows that pleasurable experience is an essential part of staying healthy. For example, in his book, *Adaptation to Life*, George Vaillant showed that, contrary to what one might expect, executives who went highest on the career ladder were those who took the most vacation time. Ornstein and Sobel show that indulging the senses through good food, beautiful scenery, pleasant scents, massages, and so on, seems to have beneficial effects on mind and body (including the immune system). In other words, the pursuit of pleasure is as valid a component of good health as eating a healthy diet and getting adequate exercise.

So, now that you have "permission" to seek pleasurable experiences, how does this relate to accommodation? The answer is that you can consider pleasure to be a resource for dealing with upset and suicidal thoughts, much as distraction or relaxation.

You might ask yourself, "What would I do for a dear friend who felt so rotten that she was doubting that life was worth living?" Chances are, your answer would be to treat her kindly. You might treat her to dinner, talk to her reassuringly, give her a gift, or take her to a movie to get her mind off things. Now ask yourself, "What do I do for *myself* when I'm feeling really rotten?" Chances are, "treat myself kindly" is not among the first answers that spring to mind. Why is this? One reason is that society is not exactly forthcoming with encouragement for "indulging" ourselves. In fact, we are often told that any such "pampering" is selfish. Now might be a good time to rethink this idea and view it as exactly what it is, namely, a dysfunctional belief. Any belief that blocks people from a healthy course of action that can make them feel better can hardly be considered anything other than dysfunctional.

To make the pursuit of pleasure an integral part of your life, you might begin by taking inventory of what brings you pleasure. On a sheet of paper, consider each of your five senses separately: the kinds of things you most like to look at, your favorite smells, the kinds of touch that feel best to you. Remember, you need not buy expensive perfume in order to treat your sense of smell (although splurging a bit is a very nice way of being a friend to yourself). Incense, for example, is an inexpensive and often overlooked way to bring pleasure into your day. Taking the time to listen to a symphony on the radio or simply sitting and watching the sun go down are other economical ways to feast your senses.

After listing ways to please each of your five senses, you might add a list of favorite activities that involve several senses. Are you allowing enough opportunity to visit with friends, participate in sports without pressure to win, visit museums or amusement parks, or pursue your favorite hobby? To get fully into this mind-set, imagine two parts of yourself having a conversation, one a childlike part, the other the good parent, who asks, "What would you like to do today? How can we have fun?"

A couple of caveats: First, it is important that you actually *write these things down* and put the lists in a place where you can find them during a period of upset. As the saying goes, the sky diver doesn't begin sewing his parachute while free-falling from an airplane. Second, be alert for unproductive thoughts about doing things for yourself. It is amazing how many people in our society believe that doing something for yourself is selfish or that buying a gift for yourself is evidence that you are somehow too flawed to find someone to buy one for you.

By the same token, many depressed people think that only losers act as best friends toward themselves. If you tend toward low self-esteem, you might begin to notice thoughts like, "If I weren't such a reject, I wouldn't have to buy perfume for myself." Nothing could be further from the truth. As a matter of fact, intelligent self-interest makes you anything but a loser. This is not an either/or situation. You can take care of yourself *and* have good friends. And if you have a shortage of rewarding relationships in your life, it becomes even more important that you treat yourself well. By pursuing pleasure for yourself, you can prevent negative thinking from robbing you of your power to make life better for yourself.

9

Step Five: Solve Your Problems without Dying

My problems have gotten out of control. The only way to solve them is to kill myself.

I can't deal with all my problems. I'm better off dead.

The problem is *me*. If I die, everyone will be fine.

I feel overwhelmed by everything. The only way out is to kill myself.

If I kill myself, I won't have to deal with the mess I've made of my life anymore.

These are some typical thoughts and comments of people who have given up on ever being able to manage life's problems. They have convinced themselves that their best option—perhaps their only option—is to kill themselves, thereby ridding themselves of all earthly concerns. What all these thoughts have in common is the mistaken belief that death is a viable solution to problems. They imply that life is one huge mess and that death sweeps it all away.

It is sometimes said that suicide is the "solution to end all problems." In reality, *suicide is the problem to end all solutions*. Viewing suicide as a solution to life's problems makes about as much sense as saying that if a house has a leaky roof and an inefficient furnace, the solution is to demolish the entire house. It is comparable to saying that the solution to world hunger is to let everyone who is hungry starve, thus ending the condition. It is all-or-none thinking at its most dangerous. It is the kind of thinking that seduces you into believing that problems can be handled only through destructive, violent means, such as suicide. It is the kind of thinking that blinds you to the peaceful solutions—the kinds of solutions that this world so desperately needs—on a grand scale and on an individual one as well.

When people believe that the only solution is death, it is because they cannot see how it will be possible to cope with life's problems. They hopelessly accept the notion that they are incapable of helping themselves. They demean themselves by insisting that they do not have the ability to think things through in order to find answers to problems.

In this chapter, we dispute the idea that death solves problems. We believe that problems can be dealt with best by staying alive, because it is always possible to improve your problem-solving skills. In this way, desperation can be turned into damage control, helplessness can be converted to empowerment, and the urge to die can be replaced with the desire to get through difficult times so that you can live better in the future.

In previous chapters, we have explained how you can make your life more worth living by making changes at any of three places: A (the situation), B (how you think about the situation), or C (how you end up feeling and behaving). Now that we have looked at ways to change Bs by changing beliefs and Cs by coping with upset (in chapters 7 and 8, respectively), let us turn to ways to make changes at A. This chapter could be subtitled "You *Can* Change the World."

Are You Underestimating Your Ability to Solve Problems?

I'm at a total loss as to what to do.

I can't take it anymore.

I can't deal with anything anymore.

I might as well do whatever I feel like doing, because nothing I do matters anyway.

I already blew it, so I might as well blow it all the way.

These are the sorts of comments that people make when they believe that their problems are out of their control. Such comments are harmful because they discourage people from trying to help themselves. In fact, they sometimes give people "permission" to make things even worse.

Another thing these self-statements have in common is that they convey a lack of respect for the individual's own ability to cope, to think clearly, and to show grace under pressure. Of course, it can be quite difficult to think rationally and constructively when you are depressed and stressed. But, believe it or not, you already possess some of the necessary qualities to address and solve some or most of your problems. You may simply be underestimating yourself and therefore giving up much too quickly.

Have You Helped Other
People Solve Their Problems?

One way to examine your problem-solving abilities is to think about the times you have given advice to other people. Sometimes we show greater skill in solving other people's problems than in dealing with our own. Therapists know this from their own experience: This is why it is a wise practice for mental health professionals to occasionally seek the counsel of other mental health professionals.

You, too, may have the ability to be objective and levelheaded when someone comes to you for counsel. If so, this indicates that you have potential as a problem solver.

You may ask yourself, "How can it be that I can help someone else, but I can't seem to help myself?" Here are a few reasons:

- It is difficult to be objective about your own problems. Most reasonably caring, intelligent people can be at least somewhat objective in helping someone else. This is good, because objectivity is one of the keys to successful problem solving. It is often necessary to examine your own problems through the eyes of others (for example, get advice, consultation, therapy) and by getting some time and distance away from the problem in order to gain perspective (for example, slow down, take your time, take a break, or sleep on it to see how things look tomorrow).

- When the problem is yours, your depressive thinking tends to magnify its worst aspects while minimizing your sense of hope. You panic, or get desperate, or become listless, and the problem persists or gets worse. When the problem belongs to someone else, you can use the powers of your adaptive thinking relatively free from depressive distortions. Therefore, you bring the "real you" to the drawing board, not the "frantic you."

- Guess what? You may actually be no less adept at handling your own problems than anyone else's, but you are simply *underestimating* your problem-solving skills in the same way that you undervalue many other aspects of yourself. You may be convinced that there is nothing you can do and that there is no point in thinking about solutions to "hopeless" situations. In spite of this, you may have the answers at your fingertips, if only you would believe in yourself, just for as much time as it would take to address the issue with gusto.

- Sometimes you are willing and able to find a good solution to someone else's difficulties because (when it comes to the other guy) "good" is good enough. However, when it comes to your own problem, you find that you have extremely high standards. "Good" is no longer good enough. You want to find the solution to end all solutions. This sort of perfectionism limits what you can realistically accomplish, and you become disillusioned. You then might consider suicide. Ironically, having perfectionistic standards means that at some level you have great faith in your capabilities and worthiness. Yet you are willing to kill yourself—the single most invalidating act imaginable—in the service of this supposedly high expectation.

Exercise 7: Recognizing Times When You Have Helped Others

This exercise invites you to review some of the situations and times in your life when you helped others. Think of some of the people who came to you for moral support or guidance in solving a problem. If you reach deep into your memory, you might be surprised by just how many times you have served in the capacity of advisor or counselor for another person.

Have You Solved Your Own Problems in the Past?

Now that you have seen how to learn from the way you have dealt with other people's problems, go a step further and study the ways that you have coped with your own problems in the past. We will assume that your life has not been easy; that you did not become suicidal "out of the blue." It is more likely that you have had to wrestle with many problems in your life just to reach this point; and yet here you are. How did you survive until now? What have you done to manage your problems in the past?

Our purpose here is not to focus your attention on bad memories in order to "learn from your mistakes." Instead, think back to times when you believed you had reached the end of your rope, but somehow, you found the wisdom, courage, and good fortune to get through. Ask yourself, "How did I do it?" The answers are probably applicable to your life today (classes in the "School of Hard Knocks" almost always have practical applications to your future life, unlike many other classes you may have taken).

Exercise 8: Recognizing Times When You Have Helped Yourself

This exercise (p. 130) provides a structured way for you to examine the successes you have had in surviving crises and solving problems. First, recall several situations in your life in which you experienced significant problems, whether related to school, jobs, relationships with others, or anything else. Next, recall your initial reactions: Did you think you were going to be okay, or did you believe that there would be no adequate solution? Then write about what you did to survive and perhaps even succeed (do not settle

---

Exercise 7: Times I Have
Helped Others Solve Their Problems

Part A: Cast of Characters in Your Life

List names of people you have helped with problem solving and the type of problem you helped them with.

1. Parent or other older relative

Name: Problem:

Name: Problem:

2. Sibling or half-sibling

Name: Problem:

Name: Problem:

3. Spouse and significant others

Name: Problem:

Name: Problem:

4. Child or other younger relative

Name: Problem:

Name: Problem:

5. In-laws and other relatives

Name: Problem:

Name: Problem:

6. Friends

Name: Problem:

Name: Problem:

7. Neighbors and other acquaintances

Name: Problem:

Name: Problem:

8. Coworkers/colleagues

Name: Problem:

Name: Problem:

9. Others (students, employees, clients)

Name: Problem:

Name: Problem:

Count the people listed above and write the number here: _____
*This is a conservative estimate of the number of people to whom you have
given advice or helped to solve a problem.*

Part B: How You Helped People Solve Their Problems

*Choose at least three people or examples from Part A and summarize as
follows:*

Name:

Problem:

What you said or did to help solve the problem:

Name:

Problem:

What you said or did to help solve the problem:

Name:

Problem:

What you said or did to help solve the problem:

Exercise 8: How Have You Solved Your Own Problems in the Past?

Situation (Date, place, event, etc.)	Thoughts & Emotions (Positive and Negative)	Actions (Coping)	Results (Your doing)
1.			
2.			
3.			

for "Things got better," because problems usually do not solve themselves— people solve problems). Finally, review how things turned out in the end and how the actual resolution of the problem compared to the catastrophe that you expected would take place.

At first, you will probably find it difficult to remember times when you coped well and solved problems. This might be because of a memory bias that is part of being depressed. Your recollections tend to focus selectively on the events consistent with the view that your life is one big problem but ignore the situations that would give you reason to feel pride and hope were you not depressed. Strive to overcome this memory bias by searching your memory, reviewing your diary, or talking to others who know you. With effort, you likely will be surprised at how many past experiences of success-ful problem solving you have forgotten or overlooked.

After completing Exercise 8, see if you notice a boost in your sense of competence to solve problems. If you do not, you may be taking your posi-tive memories for granted, thinking, "It's no big deal. Anybody could have done it in my situation." You may be saying to yourself that you coped well because you had no choice. This is called "disqualifying the positive," be-cause you are not giving yourself the credit that you deserve—credit that is based on fact, not just opinion. The fact is that you *did* have a choice. You could have given up, or made things worse, or literally lain down and died. But you didn't: You fought, and you hung in there, and you got through. This is extremely important. It shows that you have the ability to deal with problems constructively, provided you put yourself in the proper mind-set.

You might also be inclined to give credit for your survival to other people or to circumstances. You might think things such as, "I never would have made it if it weren't for my sister," or "My Higher Power lifted me up from my despair and took care of me," or "It was by sheer luck that I got by." These statements may be partially true, but they do not tell the whole story. No one else can help you unless you are part of the process. Your willingness to trust in others and yourself is necessary in order to let any-body else be there for you. Luck alone is of little use to you unless you are ready to take advantage of it. Positive experiences will in a sense go to waste unless you notice them, act on them, and feel you are deserving.

In sum, when you rebound from crises, it is guaranteed that you had something to do with it. It is vitally important that you try to understand precisely what it was that you did, thought, and felt that enabled you to help yourself and made you willing to accept assistance from others. This knowledge will have practical applications for your life *now*.

Ingredients of Good Problem Solving and How to Do It

The first step in becoming a more effective problem solver is to acknowledge that you have some problems and that feeling suicidal, far from being a solution, is *the biggest problem of them all.* It is possible to deal with the big problem (being suicidal) at the same time you are handling the other problems that collectively have pushed you to the brink.

In Chapter 5, we talked about how to survive a suicidal crisis. We reviewed some of the things you have to do in order to live to fight another day. However, this is but the first step. No one wants merely to survive desperate feelings and situations every day of his or her life. The goal is to improve the quality of life as well, so that you will be thankful that you chose to live. To achieve this end, it will be necessary to become highly practiced at dealing with the problems behind your depression and suicidality. In the following sections, we discuss the five essential ingredients of effective problem solving: (1) adopting the problem-solving mind-set, (2) defining the problem, (3) generating alternatives and plans, (4) evaluating and deciding on a course of action, and (5) taking action and appraising the results.

The Problem-Solving Mind-Set

You might be surprised to learn that ineffective problem solving is not always the result of poor problem-solving skills. Sometimes what hampers us from solving our problems is little more than a counterproductive attitude about having problems in the first place. How many times have you heard yourself say, "I can't *believe* this is happening to me!" or "It's *awful* that my life has to be so hard!" The more often thoughts like these crop up, the less likely it is that effective problem solving will follow, because such statements reflect an attitude that insists that problems should not or must not exist, or even attempts to deny that the problems exist at all.

Effective problem solving takes place in the context of an attitude of *acceptance.* The word *acceptance* as used here does not mean hopeless resignation that nothing can be done, but rather that problems do come into our lives, there is no reason why they "shouldn't," and it is our responsibility and no one else's to do something about them.

Examine the following viewpoints. How often do you adopt these attitudes when you run into difficulty, and to what degree do you believe them?

1. I have some difficult problems, but this is not unique to me. It's part of life and part of being a human being.

2. Although my problems sometimes feel overwhelming, I can make them more manageable by carefully taking stock of my situation and by defining exactly what the problems are.

3. There may not be a perfect solution to my problems, but there probably are some "good enough" answers. I need to study the situation closely in order to find them.

4. I may not be able to resolve my issues today or tomorrow, but by keeping my cool and staying constructive, I can start a positive

trend in my life. This will help me improve my life situation down the road.

5. I do not have to endure my plight alone and in silence. I can consult with the people in my life whose opinions I value highly. It is not a sign of weakness if I make use of my personal resources in this way.

6. I need not be ashamed of my problems. In fact, others will take their cue from me. If I present myself with confidence and an air of self-acceptance, others will be more apt to have faith in me as well.

7. I can start taking constructive steps to solve my problems today. I would like to see positive results as soon as possible, but I will have patience if I don't.

8. If I start to panic or catastrophize, I can remind myself to return to problem-solving mode.

9. Doing desperate things is almost never the answer. In fact, it usually makes things worse. Instead, I will think things through carefully, and I will not do anything extreme.

10. Every problem with which I have to deal is a learning experience from which I can benefit. It can make me become wiser, not just older.

These viewpoints constitute the heart of a good problem-solving mind-set. What were your automatic reactions when you read each item? How reasonable did the items seem? Were you skeptical that they could be applied to you?

You don't have to fully believe all of these self-statements to begin using them. Just by reading them, writing them in a notebook, or saying them aloud, you will begin to orient yourself toward a healthy problem-solving mind-set. In fact, we encourage you to add your own versions of these statements; but remember, they must be constructive, supportive, and in the spirit of overcoming difficulties.

Defining the Problem

In order to begin dealing effectively with a problem that is contributing to your distress, it is crucial to know exactly what the problem is. This may sound obvious; but when people feel overwhelmed by their problems, perhaps to the point of being suicidal, they often do not have a firm grasp on precisely what is wrong. They make sweeping but unclear statements such as, "Everything is falling apart," or "My entire life is a shambles," or "Nothing is going right for me." These kinds of thoughts and comments will make a person feel worse, and they won't do anything to help clarify what specifically is wrong. They certainly won't help the person begin to make changes.

To get started in the right direction, you will need to *define the problem as clearly and specifically as you can*. This requires some organized thinking and is best done by sitting down and writing.

You may be thinking, "Won't all this focusing on my problems just make me even more depressed and suicidal?" If your thinking is overgeneralized ("Everything is going wrong"), judgmental toward yourself ("I am fatally flawed and deserve to die"), or hopeless in tone ("Things will never, ever get better"), the answer might well be "yes." This could be what you are already doing and is a significant problem in itself.

However, if your thinking is specific, concrete, nonjudgmental, and makes no suppositions about the future, it will be *helpful* for you to outline a list of problems to address. To help you get started, the following are examples of helpful and unhelpful ways to define problems. We begin with "How-Not-Tos" and then follow by showing you "How Tos" define the same problems a more effectively. Compare and contrast the two methods.

How *Not* to Define Your Problems

1. Nobody loves me.

2. I'm an addict and I'll always be an addict.

3. Nothing I do works out.

4. I'm hopeless.

5. Bad things keep happening to me all the time.

6. People always take advantage of me and hurt me.

7. I can't deal with the pain of life.

8. Nothing makes me happy. I can't appreciate anything.

Defining the same problems in a constructive way:

1. I am dissatisfied with my relationships. I want to understand what I can do to improve them. I want to be able to accept people's caring and be able to return it. I don't want to stay preoccupied only with those people who care least.

2. I have an addiction that is proving difficult to overcome on my own. I want to know what it takes to survive and be content without my substance of choice.

3. I am not as successful as I would like to be. I am often at a loss to understand why my plans so often don't pan out the way I thought they would. I want to be a better planner and to make changes in my attitudes and habits so I can get more of my needs met in life.

4. I have a hard time seeing how my moods and my outlook on life can ever improve. I tend to be cynical and have too many doubts. I

often give up before I really see what can happen. I want to able to keep an open mind about changing my life and to have the courage and know-how to try to do things differently in the future.

5. I have gone through some extremely difficult times—more than my fair share—and I feel bitter about this. I feel so bitter that I tend to give up or blame others, but this just keeps me stuck in an unhappy life. I want to be able to create some good things in my life, instead of waiting around for the next disaster. I certainly want to stop doing the things that set me up for trouble.

6. I often feel victimized by other people. This is partly because I don't assert myself and partly because I tend to gravitate toward strong people who push me around. I need to learn to speak up for myself, and I need to spend more time with people who are less demanding.

7. Sometimes I get so depressed it actually hurts physically. This is my cue that I must make changes in my life. I need to find meaningful things to do and supportive people with whom to spend my time. Maybe I should consult a therapist, and maybe I am a good candidate for medication.

8. I feel so numb and disconnected. I used to be able to enjoy things, but I don't seem to feel that way now. I have to get involved in things again. I have to stop using alcohol as a crutch to get through the day, because it serves only to make me feel more in a haze. I have to be with people and maybe get counseling as well. Maybe a support group is the way to go.

You might have noticed that the constructive problem definitions are more specific, more hopeful, more clear, and less judgmental than the typical ways that depressed and suicidal persons define their problems. Each definition also lists at least one goal or possible solution. Yes, it takes some effortful thinking, but it also puts you on the right track toward finding remedies. In order to do this, *it is essential that you sit down and write (or type).* Take your time. Try not to feel pressured or rushed. Think things through methodically and calmly. This will enable you to go on to the next step in problem solving—generating alternatives and plans.

Generating Alternatives and Plans

When we find ourselves in troubling situations in life, we sometimes throw up our hands and ask ourselves the NRQ (negative rhetorical question), "What am I going to do now?" Such a question implies that there is nothing we can do and that the situation is hopeless. By contrast, if we ask this same question as a PLQ (positive literal question), we can begin the process of finding solutions.

Start by using the brainstorming technique introduced in Chapter 8. Let your imagination run free to picture as many ways as possible to deal with the problems, regardless of how implausible they may seem at first. In other words, don't prematurely censor your ideas. Don't say, "I could try this solution ... nah, that wouldn't work," or "Maybe I could ... nah, I couldn't," or "Perhaps if I talk to someone ... nah, that wouldn't work ... oh well, forget it, never mind." Instead, write down every solution that comes to mind. You can eliminate the less doable choices later. For now, let the ideas flow.

For example, let's review the first problem from the previous section. The problem was at first poorly defined as "Nobody loves me." Then it was better defined as a problem of not accepting some people's caring and of entering into relationships with people who are not adept at caring. Your job is to brainstorm some responses to this problem. The following are some examples (remember, some of these items not as good as others, because we are brainstorming and not censoring).

- I could try not contradicting someone who compliments me. Instead, I could return the compliment.

- If somebody seems to like me, I could stop assuming automatically that something must be wrong with him or her.

- I could stop saying things such as "I know you're going to leave me someday," to my spouse. Instead, I could suggest doing something enjoyable as a couple today.

- I could say, "I *am* worthy of love," to myself, at least five times when I get up in the morning and every time I look in a mirror.

- I could go to an Alcoholics Anonymous meeting, and I could keep going to meetings until I find a group whose members are particularly supportive and giving.

- I could stop calling my ex-lover (ex-spouse, etc.), because this is just a setup for rejection. Instead, I could call or write to a friend, and I won't let self-consciousness get in the way.

- I could seek fellowship at a church or other religious organization.

- I could make a collage of photos of as many people as I can think of who have cared for me in my life.

- I could strive to *act* like a lovable person. That means I would not yell at people, would cut down on profanity, and I would not always keep my door shut at work. I could volunteer to be helpful, and I could look for kind things to say. I could be persistent in doing this for months, because it might take some time for people to catch on to the "new me."

- I could not let one particular person who does not love me make me feel as if *nobody* loves me. If I feel unloved by somebody who I wish loved me, I could not despair. Instead, in order to keep from descending into a depression, I could picture in my mind's eye a number of people who do care about me.

This list could go on and on; and the more ideas you have, the better your chances are of finding solutions to your problems. On the other hand, you are under no obligation to enact all of your ideas. You get to decide which, if any, and in which order, you will choose to do. This brings us to the next step—evaluating each choice and making decisions.

Evaluating and Deciding on a Course of Action

How will you know which idea to choose? First, review all of your brainstormed ideas, item by item. Choose two or three of them that seem most reasonable at this time. Reserve the rest of your choices for later.

Second, consider the *pros and cons* of each idea and write them down. As you consider the advantages and disadvantages, be sure to think about your *long-term* goals. Do not simply do what will make you feel good right this instant but might cause trouble later. Similarly, do not avoid things that will be helpful later just because they seem hard to do now. Think of the "big picture" of your life. Take action in such a way that it will have durable, positive impact. Also, consider the effect that each of your proposed choices will have on the people who are closest to you in your life. After all, your actions have implications for them as well.

Third, when you have spelled out all of the pros and cons, choose a course of action to try first. Think about how you will go about doing what you have chosen to do. Walk through it in your mind's eye, and do this a few times. This technique is called *cognitive rehearsal*, which helps you to get organized and better prepared to enact your plan.

Let's continue with the same example. Remember, the problem at first was ill-defined as "Nobody loves me." Then, it was better defined as a problem with relationships, including difficulties in accepting care and a tendency to dwell on the people who have been a negative influence. Then, a number of alternatives were brainstormed. Next, we review them all (without censoring) and choose three possible courses of action that seem reasonable to enact at this time. Beneath each choice, we list some of the pros and cons.

Alternative 1: I could try not contradicting someone who compliments me. Instead, I could return the compliment.

Pros:
1. I would appear more confident and less shy.
2. It would make the other person feel appreciated.

3. It would let people know that I am approachable.
4. I might actually start to believe the compliments after a while.

Cons:

1. I might seem conceited.
2. Others might think I am just giving an obligatory compliment.
3. I might not know what to say, and I'll look silly.

Alternative 2: I could make a collage of as many people as I can think of who have cared for me in my life.

Pros:

1. It would remind me about good times I have had with others.
2. It might motivate me to make some long overdue phone calls.
3. It would stop me from believing that nobody cares about me.

Cons:

1. It might make me even more depressed, seeing all those photos.
2. It might remind me of all the people I have lost.
3. I might find painful reminders while I rummage through things.
4. It would take too long, and I don't have the time.

Alternative 3: I could seek fellowship at a church or other religious organization.

Pros:

1. It would be a place to meet unrowdy people.
2. It might increase my spirituality and faith as well.

Cons:

1. I wouldn't know anybody at first and I'd feel isolated.
2. I would feel like a hypocrite, because I am not religious.
3. It would make me feel guilty, because I have done bad things.
4. I might be forced to socialize and answer personal questions.

By evaluating the pros and cons, it becomes clear that, for this particular hypothetical person, the first idea is best. Accepting and returning compliments has more pros than cons and seems more immediately doable than the alternatives.

The other choices may still be very good ones. You might have noticed that the cons of each are laden with a lot of negative assumptions that may or may not be true. Therefore, in addition to choosing and enacting the course of action that has the best ratio of pros to cons, you should also evaluate whether the cons of the other choices really are likely to happen. It is quite possible that depressive thinking is still getting in the way of viable problem-solving options.

Meanwhile, it is essential to start enacting the plan. At first glance, it might not seem that taking and receiving compliments is going to amount to feeling loved. The key is in realizing that changes are necessary and that this is a reasonable place to begin. Major good things are built on top of minor good things. Even little habits such as taking and receiving compliments can start a positive feedback loop between you and others. This can ultimately result in more meaningful shifts in the way you relate to others.

Remember, this is but one option. Once you have put this plan into operation, you can go back and look at some of your other ideas. With each new response you try, you become more confident to try others. This is an essential part of positive change.

Taking Action and Appraising the Results

Now you are ready for the part of problem solving known as *behavioral experimentation*. This is a fancy way of saying, "Try it, see what happens, and compare it to what you originally expected would happen."

You may have noticed that there are times when you know what to do, and you know how to do it, but you don't do it. Why is this so? Often, it is because you expect that it won't do any good. In fact, you may even anticipate that it will make things worse. Obviously, this way of looking at things is an impediment to solving problems. It just keeps you "doin' what you're doin', and gettin' what you're gettin'." Nothing changes. You're stuck.

To overcome your reluctance to change, you have to feel as if you have some control over the situation. One useful way to accomplish this is to set up a "behavioral experiment." You make a prediction about what will happen if you try something new, such as accepting and giving compliments. Your prediction could be something such as "I will feel foolish, I will get tongue-tied, and the other person will crack a joke about me. Then I'll want to hide, or worse—I'll want to die." Write this prediction on paper, and seal it in an envelope marked "Not to Be Opened until after I Complete My Task."

No matter what happens, you have taken some control over the situation because you are running a little experiment. You have a course of action and a prediction, and now you are going to test the prediction by doing the task.

At this point, you will commit to accepting and giving compliments for a particular length of time—a week is usually a good time frame. Then, you will observe a number of results, including:

1. How you feel when you do it

2. What you are thinking when you do it

3. How the other person reacts to you

4. How you feel as the week progresses

After a week, you will have made an important behavioral change, and you will have collected evidence that will support or refute your prediction. Now go ahead and open your sealed envelope. How does your prediction compare with the reality?

If the reality is better than you predicted (for example, if other people become more inclined to talk to you, and you feel better), you have shown yourself that change can be more beneficial and less risky than you thought. If the reality is closer to what you expected (for example, you felt awkward and nobody treated you any differently), then it is time to go back a few steps. It is time to examine what went wrong. Did you have a well-formulated plan? Did you rehearse it properly in your mind's eye? Did you undermine yourself in some way? Are you looking only at what made it awkward and blinding yourself to the benefits?

After you have examined the results of your behavioral experiment, you may now go back and try it a different way, or you may choose to move on to the next behavioral experiment.

Accepting Less-than-Perfect Results

Problem solving works. It doesn't always work out as well as you might hope, but it's infinitely better than giving up and giving in. Perhaps most important, problem solving helps your life if you stay away from the following two extreme points of view:

- Nothing I do will ever make a difference, so why bother?

- If my attempts to solve my problems do not produce perfect results every time, they are a waste of time and a total failure.

Problem solving is similar to most other good things in life—sometimes it works, sometimes it doesn't, sometimes it helps a little, sometimes it prepares you for better things later—but it is not guaranteed to work every time. Nevertheless, it is part of gaining valuable life experience, even from painful events.

To be in problem-solving mode means that you are ready to tackle obstacles with determination. It means that you will keep trying if things don't go well the first time but that you will make adjustments—you will not simply do the same thing over and over again. It means that you will refuse to be a victim of your own pessimistic thinking. It means that you will keep your wits about you, even if others around you are losing theirs. It means you have a chance to live and grow and be happier, because you are exerting some positive control over your life. It means you are fighting against the idea that you are helpless against the Fates and that you are destined to suffer. Problem solving puts you in the driver's seat. If you cultivate a positive spirit and a well-constructed plan, you will be surprised at what you can accomplish.

10

Other Skills to Enhance Your Life

Throughout this book, we have tried to show you that life is worth living and that you can overcome your wish to die. We also have endeavored to show you that the process of reinvesting in life is not simply a matter of "willing" yourself to live. Instead, it involves changing your outlook, your actions, your relationships, your plans, and the way you make choices. This may seem overwhelming, but the rewards are substantial. Life should not be something simply to endure; it should be something that you can value and treasure, even if it is sometimes a struggle. This requires a new approach.

Earlier, we discussed ways you can cope with emotional pain more effectively, strategies for changing your thinking style so it is less depressive, and methods for solving problems that otherwise would seem too burdensome to bear. Now we will discuss some other methods for changing your life for the better. We will break these skills down into three major categories: assertiveness skills, relationship-enhancement skills, and "vital involvement" in life.

Entire books have been written on these subjects. For the purposes of this book, we will summarize the main points and suggest further readings if you should wish to pursue them further.

Assertiveness

Do you often get the feeling you're not being heard? Perhaps you want someone to give you back your book or repay some money you lent them, but you can't get yourself to say this directly. Perhaps you want someone to express more affection to you or stop doing or saying things that you find hurtful. Or perhaps you are in tremendous emotional pain, feeling empty or abandoned, but simply don't know how to express it. These are all places where assertiveness skills are essential.

It is nearly impossible to get your needs met if you don't express them. This sounds simple in theory; but in practice, the act of making your feelings, thoughts, and wishes known can be difficult. You might worry that you will be rejected, scoffed at, patronized, put down, or ignored. You may worry that by expressing yourself you will seem pushy or will be disliked. You may even predict that you will become too vulnerable and that people will deliberately take advantage of you if they know how you feel. These fears make the act of asserting yourself seem very challenging and may lead you to avoid asserting yourself altogether.

Despite the difficulties, it is worth taking the time and energy to develop the skills involved in expressing your wishes to others. By doing so, you will probably find that you feel more confident, more in control, and more apt to influence others to treat you with greater consideration. When such changes begin to take place, life becomes a little easier and friendlier.

To illustrate, let's consider "Sandi," a 42-year-old divorced mother of three adolescent boys, who works full-time as a legal secretary. To most observers, there is nothing unusual about Sandi. She manages her family and work responsibilities admirably and seems to get along reasonably well with others. She is also plagued by thoughts of wanting to die, because life exhausts her and appears to give her very little joy or hope in return.

How can this be? How can a "typical" person such as Sandi be suicidal? Although the complete answer to this question is too involved for the purposes of this example to discuss here completely, a partial response has to do with the harmful consequences of her unassertiveness.

Sandi is someone who quietly does all of the things that she thinks she is "supposed" to do and does not complain, no matter how burdened or unfairly treated she feels. One clear result of this pattern is that she feels dominated and mistreated by the men in her life—her boss, her sons, and her ex-husband (her deceased father was also "powerful and critical," in Sandi's view). Owing in part to her unassertiveness, Sandi believes she has no alternative but to obey their every demand, lest she feel guilty and "bad" for not doing what she "should" do.

However, when she spends all of her time and energy trying to please everyone else under the perceived threat of devaluation, Sandi leaves no time for getting her own needs met. She is lonely, fearful, tired, and very depressed (though she hides this latter condition behind a facade of calmness). Ultimately, Sandi made a serious suicide attempt by ingesting a large quantity of over-the-counter analgesic medication. Everybody in her life was shocked.

Sandi's case illustrates the harmful effects of habitually keeping your thoughts and feelings to yourself. Sandi was unable to share her feelings with those closest to her, fearing that she would be perceived as a complainer or that she would trigger angry responses. She could not reduce the demands imposed on her by her sons and boss because she could not bring herself to tell them that she needed a break, some empathy, and some cooperation.

As her stress, fatigue, and loneliness increased, Sandi's depression deepened. At this point, Sandi's lack of assertiveness contributed to the most extreme hazard of all—*she could not bring herself to ask directly for help.* Although Sandi joked about needing to see a shrink, she did not spell out the depths of her despair. Sandi did not seek professional help on her own, nor did she express sufficient distress so that others might intervene on her behalf. In the end, Sandi made a suicide attempt, a tragic way for an unassertive person to make her needs known to others.

As this example illustrates, suffering in silence prevents problems from being solved. And using attempted suicide as a cry for help is highly dangerous and ineffective in the long run. Suffering in silence and attempting suicide are two extreme, maladaptive forms of dealing with your needs. Good mental health lies somewhere in the middle and means making your wishes and feelings known to others. It involves recognizing when you are in distress and communicating your wishes and needs to others.

Before leaving the subject of assertiveness, it is important to note that even expert assertive behavior does not always succeed. There may be times when you try to tell people what you need, and for whatever reason, they do not respond. These are times to firmly resist any urge to do something drastic, such as hurting yourself, in order to send a wake-up call. Instead, you must remain flexible and seek other ways to take care of yourself. This might mean seeking therapy or joining a support group. At other times, it might be as simple as lightening your schedule, calling some friends, or saying no to someone's unreasonable demands. In more serious situations, it may mean leaving a job or a relationship in order to survive. Remember, no matter what, *it is always better to leave a job or a relationship than it is to leave life altogether.*

For further reading in this important area, we suggest *Your Perfect Right*, by Robert Alberti and Michael Emmons (Impact Publishers, 1990).

Relationship-Enhancement Skills

It is practically unheard of for someone to commit suicide when he or she feels close ties to other people. More often, the suicidal individual is convinced that he or she is all alone. We have heard our suicidal patients lament, "Nobody cares about me," or "I've burned all my bridges," or "I feel so alone." There is commonly a kernel of truth to these statements, because depressed people often disengage from social activities. However, the suicidal person's belief that relationships are meaningless, or irretrievably lost, is almost always a negative distortion.

Our emotional bonds with others are part of the spice of life. There is much happiness to be reaped when we value, nurture, and engage in our relationships with those about whom we care, like, and admire. We take a giant leap toward life—and away from suicide—when we decide to invest ourselves in the world of people.

At your times of greatest despair, you may convince yourself that you do not care about others, that they do not care about you, or both. However, you need to ask yourself, "Has it always been this way?" If you think back to times when life seemed more tolerable, it is likely that you will remember that you got along better with others. Is this a coincidence? We do not think so. More than likely, you were interacting with others in a more favorable way, and your attitudes about yourself and others were probably more positive as well.

Getting along with others makes life more complete and more fulfilling, but it does take some work and know-how. Since severely depressed people tend to have significantly reduced levels of energy and concentration, it is not surprising that their social skills often decline. The loss of an important relationship can make this condition even worse, as the depressed person feels more alone than ever, yet chooses to isolate even more.

In this situation, it is important to push hard to involve yourself in the world of people, even if you don't feel like it. It is a great investment in yourself to work on becoming someone who can share positive moments with others. You will be paid back in the form of better treatment and a more positive sense of yourself.

While recognizing the complexities of forming and keeping human relationships, we would like to present a few simple suggestions for becoming more connected to others.

First, you need to *make your presence known to others*. As a famous comedian once said, "Eighty percent of success is just showing up." For example, if you habitually eat lunch by yourself in your office, make it a point to see if you can join a group that is going out. Don't worry about people seeing you as pushy. All you have to do is ask, "Mind if I join you?" The worst they can do is say "no." If so, try being the person who invites others to have lunch with you the next day. If you are at home alone, do not simply sit by the phone or pine away over an empty mailbox. Be proactive. Be the one who writes the letter or makes the call. Let others know you are thinking about them. If you are concerned that they will find your story uninteresting or depressing, focus on their story instead. Of course, if you are at the point of considering suicide, you should tell the other person how depressed you are and that you need his or her support. A true friend would be upset if you didn't speak up about how you felt.

Second, *be responsive to kind words and invitations*. If somebody says something complimentary to you, let him or her know how much you appreciate it. Do not merely shrug it off, contradict it, or wonder what the ulterior motives are. If somebody invites you to take part in a social event of some sort, accept it. Do not automatically say, "I can't." Beware also of remaining noncommittal until the last moment, at which point you avoid going, because this can make you appear uninterested. As a result, you will unintentionally teach others not to think of you when they are making plans.

You may be saying to yourself, "The problem is not that I ignore kind words and invitations. The problem is that I never *get* them." This might be patently inaccurate. You might be getting kind gestures from others but are not aware of it because you overlook the fact that others are trying to treat you nicely. Don't laugh. We see this all the time. In this case, you must make a daily effort to be alert for ways that other people reach out to you that you have not been aware of.

For example, one of our patients called in a suicidal state after getting a "terrible letter" from a long-distance lover. The therapist asked the patient if he would read the letter aloud over the phone. The letter contained numerous apologies and "I love you"s throughout. It also stated that "our relationship is strained but very important to me." When asked to summarize the basic meaning of the letter, the patient tearfully said, "She wants to dump me." The patient essentially ignored the 95 percent of the letter that showed caring and magnified and distorted the 5 percent that expressed doubts.

We have found that severely depressed people tend to make this same perceptual mistake in many of their relationships, both casual and serious. They become tone-deaf and color-blind to words and gestures of concern, care, support, and admiration. In contrast, they are acutely aware of the interpersonal discomfort or awkwardness that may exist in their relationships. They then determine that they are all alone and that nobody cares.

To combat this state of aloneness, it is important to "just say yes" when people ask you to spend time with them. This may entail socializing, collaborating on a group task, or being receptive to a phone call, letter, or friendly visit. If you habitually turn people down when they try to engage you in some way, they may come to believe either that you do not like *them* or that you would like others to respect your need for space. In the end, you will remain by yourself, a condition that is largely unconducive to overcoming a depressive condition. Before you prematurely determine that you have lost interest in people, spend some time with them, and then assess how you feel. Do not make assumptions.

If you are not overlooking people's gestures, the other possibility is that you in fact are not receiving kind words or invitations from others. In this case, you might try being proactive in *giving* sincere compliments and *extending* invitations. Such gestures are often quickly reciprocated.

A third way to enhance your interpersonal life is to *make a point of treating others with consideration and respect*. This is not to be confused with the insincere act of buttering up a person as a way to achieve an ulterior motive. We are simply suggesting that you take the approach that you will give others the attention and empathy you yourself would like to receive. Since many personal interactions are a two-way street, it is likely that some of the people you treat with kindness and liking will come around to return the sentiment. This, too, is a central factor in enhancing your relationships, as well as your life.

Our final suggestion may sound a little odd, but please bear with us. If one of your closest companions is a dog, cat, horse, or another animal, consider the factors that make that relationship so important and successful in your life. Many times, when people feel wounded by the world, they may choose instead to invest their trust and care in animal friends. This is good. It is an emotional bond with another living being, and it is likely that this being gives loyalty and unconditional love in return. Further, an attachment to a dog, cat, or other animal proves that you are capable of giving and receiving affection. The question then becomes, can you hope to attain a comparable level of quality in your relationships with other humans? If you are feeling particularly cynical, or hopeless, you would probably answer negatively. However, this may be needlessly pessimistic, especially in light of the positive lessons to be learned from relationships with animals.

What are some of these lessons? For starters, relationships with animals, however rewarding, are imperfect, just like human relationships. You get exasperated, lose patience, worry, and experience inconvenience in meeting the needs of another. However, you accept this as a tolerable cost in the context of a companionship that pays off so handsomely in other ways.

Another lesson is that ties to pets, however imperfect, are strengthened by a sense of consistency and safety. These are conditions that you can strive to achieve in your interactions with the people who mean the most to you.

Yet another lesson is that there is great value in getting close to another living being, even though the relationship will not last forever. When people devote themselves to an animal, they don't say to themselves, "My dog is probably going to die on me in ten years or so, so what is the point of getting too attached?" (Note that this is an NRQ, a negative rhetorical question.) Instead, they typically welcome the joy they experience during the course of this relationship, in spite of the probability that their loved one eventually will leave them. By accepting this, they prosper. They let themselves enjoy the relationship, and it grows. This seems quite applicable to human relationships.

Finally, for those who would say that animals have qualities that are superior to those of humans, and therefore relationships between humans can never match the level of affection and trust that people have with their pets, we would respond by indulging in a rhetorical question of our own—if this is so, why do animals become so attached to people? At the very least, those who love animals should be able to form kinships with other humans who love animals. Regardless of what you may think of humans, a bond between a person and his or her pet still involves a human element. Perhaps it brings out the best in humans—we don't know for sure. Can you tap into these characteristics in order to improve your interactions with human friends, relatives, acquaintances, coworkers, neighbors, spouses, and others? We think so, and we think it is worth a try.

"Vital Involvement"

As noted previously, Albert Ellis has shown many ways to overcome debilitating thoughts and feelings. However, it is worth noting that emotional health is more than the mere absence of emotional disturbance; and Ellis has something to say along these lines as well. In his book with Robert Harper (1975), *A New Guide to Rational Living*, he notes that many unhappy people manifest an excessive degree of self-absorption. Depressed people in particular withdraw from other people and social activities and instead become preoccupied with their problems and imperfections. As you know if you've been there, this is anything but a happy state. For most people who are self-absorbed, this serves only to magnify their feeling of inadequacy and to cause them shame about not being more involved with other people.

As a remedy, Ellis proposes "vital involvement." In contrast to self-absorption, vital involvement means that a person is less involved with him- or herself and more with *life*. As Ellis points out, "To some degree, human contentment seems almost synonymous with absorption in outside people and events . . ." (1975, p. 186).

Before proceeding to ideas for increasing your vital involvement, let us caution you against overreacting to this idea. Some misguided teachers (parents, clergypersons, etc.) may tell you that devoting *any* attention to yourself is selfish and self-centered; but as we hope you deciphered in the preceding section on assertiveness, we strongly believe that emotional health requires that you be able to take care of your own needs and interests. So suggesting that you get outside of yourself and help others, or work on community projects, in no way is meant to imply that attention to your own needs is bad. To the contrary, it appears that a *balance* of self-concern and outward-directed energy is what's best.

As a starting place for getting more vitally involved, it will be helpful to remember two general points. The first was just mentioned: Vital involvement typically means *involvement with other people*, working jointly on projects (anything from helping clean up a community park to serving as a volunteer for charitable organizations), or doing something to help other people. As we stated in Chapter 8, the latter seems to be especially beneficial, not only to the person helped, but also to the helper. This phenomenon is well recognized in the self-help movement. For many years, dating from the beginnings of Alcoholics Anonymous and before, people involved in self-help groups have noticed that when they offer assistance to other people, they themselves feel better. This is not only because they are often thanked for their efforts, but also because the process of helping shows them that they are more than just their problems—we all have strengths that we might fail to notice until we put them to work.

The second general point is that vital involvement almost always means *doing something*. Passive pursuits such as reading or watching television are fine in moderation, but human beings rarely seem happy when they feel that they are spectators on the sidelines of life, simply watching while others act. So as you think about increasing your vital involvement, think, not just about what you can be or what you can know, but about what you can *do*.

Now, where to begin? You might find yourself full of good intentions, convinced that it's a good idea to get more vitally involved, but clueless when it comes to specific ideas. Let us review a few general directions and then consider some specifics.

If you know when your depression and suicidality began, think back to the months and years before that. What did you do to fulfill your need to be vitally involved with others? What did you do that gave you pleasure but which has since fallen out of your routine? Were you actively involved in church or synagogue projects? Did you serve on the board of a community organization? Did you take care of your elderly neighbors' mail and pets when they were away? It is a well-established psychological principle that past behavior predicts future behavior, so whatever brought you a sense of connection and accomplishment in the past is likely to do so in the future as well.

Another general way to get ideas is to look to positive role models. Do you know of any friends or relatives who live life to the fullest, who seem to squeeze two days of living out of every 24-hour period? If so, then take notice of how they invest their time and energies. Talk to that brother-in-law who devotes time to Little League and the Lions Club, or that coworker who has a story to tell every Monday morning about her exploits at flea markets or with her hiking club. If you notice yourself feeling overwhelmed and having thoughts such as, "Those people are different; I would never have the energy for such things," remind yourself that energy begets energy. Most people report that as they become more active, their mood lifts and their energy level increases. In addition, the gratification derived from such activities serves as a reinforcer, increasing the probability of more activity in the future.

Use this as a behavioral experiment: For the next week, try rating both your energy level and your activity level from 0 to 100 percent, using the form in Figure 10-1. Then, do the same for the following week, except this time make a vigorous effort—even *force* yourself—to become more vitally involved, using some of the ideas in this chapter. Now compare your scores and see how your energy level compares with your level of vital involvement.

For some specific ideas on how to get vitally involved, consult Table 10-1. In it, you will find some of the activities already discussed, as well as some others for you to consider. If none of these activities are available in

Figure 10-1: Ratings of Vital Activity and Energy Levels				
Day of the Week	Typical Week (Before making changes)		After Becoming More Vitally Involved	
	Activity (0-100%)	Energy (0-100%)	Activity (0-100%)	Energy (0-100%)
Sunday				
Monday				
Tuesday				
Wednesday				
Thursday				
Friday				
Saturday				

your area, use them as a way of generating other ideas for yourself. Remember, too, that newspapers typically are chock-full of announcements from local community interest groups. Such organizations are often listed in the front of the phone book as well, under "Community Service Numbers." Finally, don't underestimate the power of brainstorming. Ask other people about how they involve themselves with others and contribute to the community. And remember always to maintain an experimental attitude. Negative prediction will only keep you isolated and unfulfilled; experimenting with new forms of vital involvement very well might bring you an assortment of pleasant surprises.

Table 10-1: Ideas for Becoming More Vitally Involved

Volunteer at your community hospital

Serve food at a soup kitchen

Coach Little League, childrens soccer, football, etc.

Join a political campaign

Join a hiking club

Serve as a Big Brother or Big Sister

Call United Way and inquire about donating your time

Become a member of the board of directors of a local agency

Join or start a Neighborhood Watch program

Shovel snow for your elderly neighbor

Call your clergyperson and ask how you can get involved

Join Lions Club, Optimist Club, Junior League, or some
other service organization

Join a club devoted to your hobby

Volunteer to teach reading skills through your local
literacy organization

PART III

Epilogue: Philosophy Is Important, Too

11

It's Okay to Get
Flowery about Life

In our modern, results-oriented society, it is popular to look askance at philosophy, perhaps viewing it as irrelevant to everyday "realities" and a luxury only to be indulged in by college students and aristocrats. We ourselves may have fallen prey to this attitude somewhat by arranging this book with the how-tos first and reserving philosophical reflection for the end. However, we hope that it is apparent throughout the book that philosophy is anything but irrelevant to the quality of daily life.

It's relevance, of course, depends on how we define *philosophy*. Much of the highly technical discourse of academic philosophy, as set forth in textbooks and professional journals, does perhaps have limited relevance to everyday life, at least in the form in which it is written. However, if you think about it, *nothing is more fundamentally philosophical than whether to live or die*. Consider Hamlet's famous soliloquy: "To be or not to be, that is the question . . ." And if suicide is a philosophical issue, then so, too, are the attitudes and beliefs that underlie suicide. A decision that you are not worthy to live, for whatever reason, is based on a philosophy (a terribly harsh one) of human worth. Similarly, a suicide based on suffering is often based on a philosophical refusal to accept certain realities of the human condition.

We believe that philosophy has *everything* to do with suicide and thus has a legitimate place in this discussion. However, as we explore philosophical issues, do not assume, as some mistakenly do, that just any philosophical view, because it is personal, is "truth." Although you have a right to feel the way you feel and believe what you believe, philosophical systems can most certainly be "wrong" in the sense that they sometimes are based on erroneous reasoning. So let us embark on a tour of philosophical attitudes toward life to see what they might offer someone who questions the meaning and value of life.

Sociocultural Views of Life

The Dark Side

The "dark" view of life is perhaps best captured by the bumper sticker that reads, "Life's a bitch and then you die." We wonder who had such a sour outlook on life to think up such a motto and how he or she got that way. But what is even more of a point to ponder is the fact that many individuals shared this point of view and chose to express it publicly. Great numbers of these bumper stickers have appeared across the country, and we wonder how many more people have a similar view but do not choose to advertise it.

Anyone who might be puzzled as to how so many people developed this negative outlook on life need only tune into the evening news for some clues. News about murders, child abuse, natural disasters, and political corruption bombard the senses. Change the channel, and you see the latest scandalous and painful discussion of who betrayed whom on *Geraldo* or the *Sally Jesse Raphael Show*. Switch channels again, and you see lawmakers in gridlock over abortion rights or budget cuts. You turn off the TV and step outside, only to be confronted with air pollution, snarled traffic, and homeless people. Suddenly, that bumper sticker starts to make more and more sense!

A Brighter Picture

How can you deal with such a bleak worldview? First, it is crucial to know that the media have a serious case of *negative filtering*. This means that they notice and dwell on the bad and overlook the good. As the saying goes, "Good news doesn't sell newspapers," and this seems to be even more true of television. You also need to know, as we pointed out earlier in this book, that depression may have given you a case of negative filtering as well. This means that you might notice only bad things about yourself, others, and the world, and the media might reinforce this bias through their constant focus on what's wrong with the world. Have you ever noticed how reporters almost always sign off on a negative note, no matter how positive the story might have been ("The stock market is at record highs, but only time will tell whether a correction is around the corner")?

Simply being aware that the media (and possibly your brain) often focus on the negative side of the picture can help you pay more attention to what's right about life. Having recognized this, the next step is to start seeking information to balance a dark worldview. (Notice we are not saying that bad news should be disregarded. Trying to block out negatives and pay attention only to positives would put you out of touch with reality and probably wouldn't feel convincing anyway.) You can start by sifting through a recent issue of *Time* or *Newsweek* specifically to make note of positive aspects of life. You will notice, for example, that the Cold War is over and that for the first time since the 1950s terrible instruments of global destruction are themselves being destroyed. You'll notice, too, that apartheid has ended in South Africa and that democracy is taking root in many places in the world (such as Central America) that had once been written off. Some things, though less obvious, are equally positive, such as the fact that lead has been almost eliminated from the air we breathe and some endangered species have been brought back from the brink of extinction. Furthermore, people are living longer than ever before, partly due to better health practices and partly because of marvelous new medical technologies.

As another part of your proactive quest for a positive worldview, you might visit your bookstore specifically to look for books that will enhance your outlook, such as Barbara Ann Kipfer's *14,000 Things to Be Happy About* or Carl Sagan's latest book on the wonders of the universe. Remember, the intent here is not to turn you into a Pollyanna, naively believing that everything is wonderful. The purpose is to develop an outlook that is *balanced*, with information about the world that represents both the good and the bad.

Table 11-1 lists some good things about life today. As you read them, pay attention to your internal dialog. Be especially on the lookout for the following pattern: "Okay, maybe polio has been conquered, but look at how many people are dying of AIDS." This comes under the heading of "disqualifying the positive" and is a self-defeating way of staying stuck in a negative worldview. When you notice yourself doing this, try turning it around, like this: "Granted, the AIDS epidemic is scary, but if we can knock out such scourges as polio and smallpox, then surely there's hope." In this way, you are deliberately shifting from a dysfunctional either/or way of thinking ("If all is not okay with the world, then life stinks") to a more realistic both/and perspective.

Choosing Life: Why Not?

If you will allow us the indulgence of heading this section with a rhetorical question, let us look at the benefits of making the active decision to go on living. Although we have often heard severely depressed people say, "I would kill myself, if only I had the courage," we believe that the decision to live is a better, more powerful, and more affirmative act of courage. We acknowledge that it does require a measure of bravery to deal with life and all of its demands. This is especially true when stressors mount, supports diminish, and life seems harsh for long periods of time. It takes strength of resolve and character to work through such times. If you have ever felt suicidal, but trudged through life nonetheless, this pertains to you.

Table 11-1: Examples of What's Right with Life Today

Reconciliation with Vietnam

Mozart and Beethoven

Ice cream

Hubble space telescope

Children's laughter

Air conditioning

Recycling

Fall colors

End of the Cold War

Families that take in foster children

Michelangelo, Renoir, and Matisse

Thanksgiving

People living longer

Dropping prices on personal computers

Criminals vastly outnumbered by honest people

The U.S. Constitution

Nuclear disarmament

Winter is always temporary

It's okay to drink the water

The miracle of life

We are not suggesting that life is something that simply must be endured. Rather, we are saying that if you can survive the rough times, life can provide wonderment, excitement, and even fulfillment. As mortals, none of us can predict with certainty when life will be kind and fair to us and when it will throw us into desperate straits. You can, however, maintain a constructive outlook on yourself and your personal world that will increase the chances that you will be prepared for the good that life has to offer, when the opportunities arise. You can resolve to be good to yourself, even when it seems that others are not so accommodating. You can give of yourself, so that you may occasionally bring a little help and happiness into the lives of others. More times than not, your positive deeds will be returned to you. You can determine that you will stay on this planet as long as you can, so that you will not rob yourself of the unforeseen, meaningful, future experiences that you would otherwise miss if you decided to die prematurely.

Real People Who Chose Life

Almost without exception, the most compelling arguments about the meaning of life—and the importance of living it—come from those who have been to the brink of death and back. We have been privileged to witness the journeys of such people and to learn from their stories. We have been inspired by their experiences, and even more, we have come to view life from many different perspectives, each of which has something valuable to teach us. These "lessons" in choosing life are illustrated in the following examples.

The Movie Maven's Metaphor

"Joel" was once a depressed, morose, lonely fellow whose only reported joy in life was in immersing himself in the viewing of old movies. Today, he is still a movie buff, but he is considerably happier than before.

Joel described a mental technique that he employed in order to survive his loneliest, most pessimistic times. He explained that one of the cardinal rules of popular Hollywood films is that the hero never dies (and if he or she does die, that person must somehow be brought back to life). He also noted that the most effective movies that portray the plight of the underdog in society create a certain kind of story line—one in which the chief character has few or no supporters within the film but generates almost unanimous support in the viewing audience.

Joel decided to adopt these movie tactics in his approach to his own depression. He dubbed himself the "hero" (or, at least, the "protagonist") and kept reminding himself that the hero doesn't die (at the very least, he would never commit suicide). More importantly, however, when Joel felt most alone, he would imagine that he had a huge throng of invisible supporters. These people existed on the other side of the silver screen, in the audience. Joel reported that this metaphor helped him greatly whenever he believed that the people in his life (that is, in the movie) did not care about him.

Joel's tactic became part of a personal philosophy in support of life, and it gave him some measure of comfort and hope. Through cognitive therapy, Joel learned how to apply this philosophy to his real (not just fantasized) life. His mission was to find and connect with his "audience." In part, this meant taking a more active role in seeking out congenial social companionship. Ironically, it also meant spending less time watching movies in isolation, as he had been wont to do. Gradually, Joel overcame his greatest inhibitions about interacting with others, and his moods improved markedly over time. Suicide became a distant thought. Life seemed easier, even promising.

The Smart Shopper's Strategy

"Jocelyn" had always been a thrifty consumer. Almost everything she purchased was at reduced price. Whenever she bought anything new, she made certain it had a good warranty or came from a store with a favorable return policy. Jocelyn earned a modest living, but her spending habits allowed her to live rather nicely, within her means. This was something in which she took pride.

Jocelyn was suicidal when she entered therapy. She viewed life as a nonstop chore that provided little or no hope for happiness. However, one of the positive turning points in her treatment came when she and her therapist reflected on the "consumerism of life and death."

In short, death is a guaranteed "commodity." Life, on the other hand, is not. Jocelyn realized that, no matter what she did, she would at some point "obtain" death. It was a sure thing. She didn't have to work for it. She didn't have to make special arrangements for it. She didn't need to "maintain" it (in the way that one might maintain a house or car so that it is maximally functional for the longest period of time).

Jocelyn also realized that she didn't need to hasten it. Even if death was a much desired thing, she didn't have to worry about it going out of production, or being sold out, or going out of style. She could wait for it, and it would always be there, waiting for her.

Life, however, needed to be handled with care. Arguably, it was a trillion-to-one shot that Jocelyn was ever born to begin with. Life was never guaranteed, and it might just as well never have happened in the first place. Additionally, Jocelyn's life was unlike anybody else's and therefore was unique and in low supply. This meant that Jocelyn's life had high market value. Further, Jocelyn's life did not come with a warranty (in this sense, the term "life insurance" is a misnomer—it should be called "early death insurance"). If it ended, she couldn't get her "money" back nor could she turn it in for another life. Therefore, proper maintenance was everything. No other commodity needed a "handle with care" logo more than life.

In this light, Jocelyn's suicidality represented poor consumerism, something which was very much at odds with her self-image as a smart shopper. Nevertheless, to be willing to let life go into disrepair, perhaps to throw it away altogether, when there was no warranty, would be foolhardy consumerism.

Similarly, to hasten the arrival of death, a product that Jocelyn was guaranteed to receive anyway, could only be construed as lacking in patience and foresight. Jocelyn had always had the patience and foresight to wait until something went on sale. This impatience for death, too, was poor shopping. Clearly, Jocelyn needed to wait until such time as death would have a lower price tag. To choose to die now, at the age of 38, would come at a huge price indeed.

Jocelyn argued that her desire to commit suicide was based on the need to escape from the pain of life, which she reportedly could bear no longer. However, when asked to review the past year of life, Jocelyn discovered that her life had not consisted of unmitigated suffering. The good times she had experienced were fleeting—indeed, this is part of the lack of guarantees inherent in life. However, if Jocelyn could have some rewarding times in the midst of the worst period of her life, what might she be forfeiting in the future if she killed herself now? This question began to haunt Jocelyn. She tentatively agreed to hang on dearly to the thing that was mysterious, unpredictable, and not guaranteed (life) and to let that which was certain (death) take its own course in its own time.

Liza's Life Imitates ER

For someone who is severely distressed, television often represents an escape from reality. Clearly, this strategy (in its excess) has numerous drawbacks, including the perpetuation of lethargy and isolation. On the other hand, once in a while, this medium can convey a hopeful message. Such was true of "Liza," who was a big fan of television's popular show about the emergency room staff in a Chicago hospital, *ER*.

One of the characters, Carol the nurse, attempts suicide in an early episode. She survives and goes on to become a central figure in the show. You may be asking, "So what? This is fiction." True, but Carol resonated with Liza in a number of ways.

First, one of Liza's life issues was a discordant and ill-fated relationship, just like Carol the nurse. Second, Liza read that the original story line was to have had Carol die, but the prescreening audience's response was so negative that the writers reconsidered, and Carol survived. Not only did she live, but she seemed to have no lingering desire to end her life, unlike many people who survive a suicide attempt.

The reason for this script reversal was that the viewing audience *liked* Carol the nurse. Liza was struck by this fact, as she had always been convinced that anyone who became aware of her depression would chastise her and reject her. Carol the nurse was well liked by millions, in spite of her suicide attempt. People liked her for who she was, regardless of her emotional difficulties. Carol had something to live for, so the writers of the show kept her alive. Liza began to wonder if this lesson could be applied to her own life.

Third, Carol's life in the aftermath of her suicide attempt was quite eventful. She still suffered through ill-fated relationships, but her life was full, interesting, and she had many meaningful connections with people. Nobody with whom she worked in the emergency room seemed to be fazed by Carol's psychiatric history. Liza felt very connected to this character and made it a point to make Carol the nurse one of her unofficial role models in life.

Sound silly? Only if we close our minds to some of the miracles of life; and believe us, getting a set of reasons to live from watching television is nothing short of a miracle. Still, it is a well-written show, with characters and situations that ring true to life. Therefore, it is not entirely a shock to find that

Liza was so deeply touched by the life of one of its characters. Liza learned, through the experiences of Carol the nurse, that she could have a meaningful life in spite of misbegotten love affairs, that she could still be loved and respected in spite of being suicidal, that life could be wonderful in the aftermath of despair, and that only Liza could write her own script; so she had better renew her contract with life before the writer had her killed off.

The Destiny of "Daniel the Devout"

"Daniel" was a suicidal patient with a heart-wrenching dilemma. He was desperately depressed and devoid of hope, and he was making arrangements in anticipation of his own demise. On one hand, he was afraid to commit suicide for fear that he would be damned for this mortal sin. On the other hand, he reasoned that he could effect his own death by being "careless" (for example, go wading out too far from shore), thus gaining access to a glorious afterlife.

Religion was central to Daniel's life and therefore was also inextricably woven into his discussions in therapy. The therapist was tempted to gain leverage in support of the choice to live simply by expounding on Daniel's fear of damnation for committing suicide. However, this was a risky and incomplete strategy, owing in part to Daniel's already having considered this problem, yet still being tempted to find a way to take his own life.

Daniel found a more compelling reason to live when he and his therapist began discussing the following topic: preparation for the next world. An analogy was drawn between the gestation period in the mother's womb and the "gestation" period on planet Earth, as each pertained to attaining viability for the next phase of existence.

In essence, Daniel understood that babies who are born prematurely have a lesser chance of survival to the degree that their arrival comes earlier and earlier in the pregnancy. For example, in spite of advances in modern medicine, it would be almost impossible for a 4-month-old fetus to survive outside of the mother's womb, and thus it would perish from "lack of viability" in this world. Daniel was asked to consider whether the same process could be applied to this life as a period of development for the afterlife? Was Daniel, at the age of 25, ready for the next phase of his eternal development? If he was meant to live to the age of 70 or beyond, would his death at age 25 make him "unviable" for the afterlife? Would he have to repeat a mortal life and therefore go back to square one? On the other hand, if he allowed his life to play itself out as it was "destined," would this represent his natural "gestation period" as a mortal and therefore make him ready for the next life? These were the questions that got Daniel to do some heavy-duty thinking before he let his current emotions rule his decision to live or die.

The result of these philosophical and theological ponderings was that Daniel decided to "let it be." He would allow life to unfold as it was meant to do. He would not impose his will to end his life. Instead, he would find a way to develop in as many positive ways as he could, so as to be "viable" for the next life.

Matthew vs. Murphy's Law

We are all familiar with Murphy's Law: "If something can go wrong, it will, and at the worst possible time." "Matthew" believed that his entire life was held hostage to the sadism of Murphy's Law. For example, just when he was good enough to make the varsity basketball team in high school, Matthew fractured his ankle and missed the entire season. When he was in college, he was the only person expelled from his dorm for possession of marijuana, even though the "entire hall had pot." Years later, when he finally decided that he was ready to commit to his girlfriend, she announced to him that she had started to date someone else seriously. The final straw occurred when Matthew turned down a potentially lucrative job that would have required him to move out of state. Weeks later, his supposedly "safe" position was eliminated, and he was left with no employment at all.

Matthew was a depressed and bitter person, believing that nothing would ever work out well for him. He entered therapy because he was thinking about suicide and knew that he needed help. Matthew wanted to believe that life could change for the better, but his run of bad luck had made him cynical. He was convinced that any glimmer of hope that might come out of therapy somehow would be cruelly snatched from him, no matter what he did, because he believed that Murphy's Law reigned supreme.

An important turning point came when Matthew and I (CN) hit on the following thought: To commit suicide would be the ultimate submission and surrender to Murphy's Law. How so, you may ask? Together, we reasoned that it would be just like Matthew to commit suicide, just before things would have improved markedly in his life. "Murphy" would have won once again, once and for all. We agreed that we could not let that happen.

At all costs, Matthew had to find a philosophy of life that would defeat Murphy's Law. In order to achieve this end, suicide had to be eliminated as an option. In its place, Matthew would have to adopt the Law of Averages. Specifically, if Matthew kept moving forward, trying the best he could, and applying all the lessons he could learn from therapy, he would have his day in the sun. However, he could not stop there, for that would be to tempt Murphy's Law to reemerge once again. Matthew would have to adopt an attitude that said, "I will not take anything for granted. I will not expect the best, and I will not fear the worst. I will simply do my best to be a self-aware person who gets joy out of every day and who tries to plan for an enjoyable tomorrow."

Each time Matthew's depressed mood would worsen, we quickly mobilized to reestablish the mind-set he had adopted to combat Murphy's Law.

Matthew reminded himself that by committing suicide he would almost surely guarantee that things would have been better, had he chosen to stay alive. He turned his bitterness toward the concept of Murphy's Law and away from life itself. At heart, he believed he was a good person, so we invoked the sports adage, "You have to be good to be lucky." This meant that it was still possible for him to have good fortune, but he had to work more on his "technique" (for example, problem solving, proactivity, planning, engaging in pleasurable activities, investing in relationships, etc.). This was the central theme of his therapy.

The Meaning of Life

Why are we here? What's it all about? What is our purpose? What good is it to try so hard to live when we're all going to die someday anyhow? Is our existence meaningful? If so, why?

These are but some of the questions that philosophers, theologians, poets, scientists, and many others have pondered for eons. We cannot hope to begin to address questions about "the meaning of life" as well or as thoroughly as the thousands of authors and millions of everyday folks who have come before us. However, we believe it is important that each of us tries to make some sense of existence in his or her own way. This is especially true when someone considers ending his or her existence as we know it.

We cannot predict the future. We cannot control every aspect of our fate. We cannot hold onto things we treasure for eternity, nor can we regain some of the dearest things we have lost. It is these facts of life, among others, that contribute to making life so hard sometimes.

On the other hand, it is an inexplicable miracle that each of us is here at all. All you have to do is consider all of the thousands of chance occurrences that had to fall into place, just so you could be born, to realize that your entrance into this world required a winning lottery ticket to one of the most exclusive clubs in the universe. This life—this chance to experience—is a gift, an opportunity, a wonder. This is so difficult to remember when you are in pain. To a person who is suffering, every moment can seem like an eternity. By the same token, to a person who grasps onto life for all it is worth, each joyous moment can be timeless as well.

We are here in this life for but a short time. We don't know what lies beyond, and we do not know if we will ever pass this way again. All we have is here and now and the hope that "here and now" will happen for at least a little while longer. We have experiences that are so important to notice: a shared laugh with a friend, the soft touch of a child's hand holding onto yours, the tickle of a beloved dog's tongue licking your cheek, the moment of discovery (eureka!) when you solve a problem, the sense of pride when people give you friendly applause, the warmth of connection with another person who wants to understand your feelings, the excitement of learning something new.

Think of the bounce of energy on awakening the morning after a restful night's sleep, the chills up your spine when a singer's performance touches your soul, the awe of watching a picturesque sunset, the serenity of sharing a quiet moment with someone you love, the adventure of arriving at a place you have never been before, the thrill of being thoroughly engrossed in an action movie, the comfort of a warm meal on a chilly day, the quiet joy of hearing kind words, the feeling of togetherness just after you and your teammates have finished a well-played game, the frightened fun of a rollercoaster ride.

Consider the satisfaction of hearing someone say thank you after you have lent a helping hand, the coziness of a warm blanket on a winter's morning, the sight of a rainbow after a summer's shower, the pleasurable relief of a splash in the pool on a hot day, the relaxed leisure of chatting with friends around the dinner table, the intellectual excitement of a fresh idea, the first day of feeling well again after a cold, being touched upon hearing that somebody said something nice about you when you weren't around, the rapture of listening to or performing a powerful piece of music, as well as many other such experiences. Consider the satisfaction of remembering and reminiscing about these times in your life and quietly hoping that you will have these feelings again in the future.

We need to be most aware of ourselves and our lives precisely at those moments when we have the kinds of experiences and feelings just described. We need to slow down and take the time to think about what is really most important in our lives. We need to take stock of how we treat ourselves and others and take a chance on being just a little kinder to both.

Although it may be true that nothing lasts forever, we can invest ourselves in things that are relatively more enduring than others—our health, our relationships, our ideas, our plans, and our daily sense of purpose, to name a few. These are among the pursuits that make life more meaningful, if not comprehensible.

It has been said that when one of us dies, a piece of all of us dies as well. We are all on this journey of life together, and it is important to all of us to keep our "team" intact for as long as natural occurrence will allow.

Although suicide at times may seem like a reasonable option when you are severely depressed and hopeless, it is in fact a forfeiture of all that could be and a severing of ties to all others, including those to whom you may have become attached in the future. Instead, let us work to make life better, rather than end it. Let those of us in the community of life band together to make life's joys a little sweeter and life's sorrows a little more tolerable, rather than split apart into the isolation that is death. As one of our earlier examples illustrated, let us "let it be."

That fact of our mortality has already been decided for us. Therefore, to decide to die by our own hand is *not* an example of taking control. Death will happen anyway. By committing suicide, all we do is take away what limited control we do have in this existence—control that we would do better to try to exert *within* our lives.

By reading this book, you have shown that you are willing to keep an open mind about your decisions regarding life and death. We are thankful that you have patiently listened to our message and that you have been willing to entertain points of view that might seem at odds with your personal experience of life. We hope that you will decide to reinvest in your time on earth and that this choice will lead to a positive ripple effect in your interactions with others, some of whom themselves may be contemplating death.

An Old Testament scripture holds that a person who saves a single life also saves an entire world. By making the active choice to live, you are in fact saving your own entire world. You may also be saving others, though you may never know who they are. They may be the student whose life you will turn around, the sibling who will thrive because of your guidance, the children and grandchildren who might yet come into existence because of your decision to live and procreate, the children and grandchildren who are already in this world who are better off for your being in their lives, the friends who will find comfort in your care during their times of need, the people in religious or 12-step groups who benefit from hearing your story of recovery and hope, and many, many others.

We have presented a number of cognitive therapy strategies in this book, in hopes that they will be of some assistance to you in your quest to help yourself or a loved one. We hope that you will make use of them. However, we respect your ability to find your own way. If there are other methods that you prefer to use to reawaken your desire to go on living, we applaud you for thinking of them and using them. Do whatever it takes—you have our support.

We hope to continue this journey of life for as long as it is meant to be, and we hope that you will choose to remain on this path along with us. Good luck.

PART IV

Appendix

A

Guide for Concerned Family Members and Friends

As noted in Chapter 1, the topic of suicide remains a rather taboo subject in our society and time. As a result, many people who are considering suicide are loath to discuss their feelings with the people in their lives who might otherwise be most concerned and anxious to know. Similarly, many people who become aware or who suspect that a friend or loved one is thinking about taking his or her own life are hesitant to express their suspicions or fears to the suicidal person. Conversely, some suicidal individuals talk at great length and with great frequency about their self-harming ideas and intentions, leading others to be anything from alarmed to constantly on guard, exasperated, or exhaustedly detached.

The upshot of these examples is that communication between suicidal persons and their friends and relatives often is deficient or problematic. At the very time when accurate, direct, facilitative communication is most needed between the deeply depressed person and others in his or her life, such communication typically is lacking. This is not to imply that it's the "fault" of one party or the other. Rather, it is to point out that an important resource—communication—needs to be attended to, worked on, and encouraged in order to maximize the chances that the suicidal person can be helped in time.

In this appendix, we address some of the questions frequently asked by friends and family members of suicidal individuals.

What Warning Signs Should I Look For?
People who experience suicidal feelings come from all walks of life, in all shapes and sizes, and have all manner of personality characteristics.

Therefore, we cannot present you with a standard profile of someone who is suicidal. It can happen to anyone.

However, there are some behavioral signs that are more common than others in identifying someone who may be suicidal. Additionally, there are some life situations that are more apt than others to trigger depression and suicidality in some people. We outline some of these signs and situations here. Some will seem obvious, but it is the obvious that is sometimes overlooked in individuals who need your help. Others may seem less apparent, but we present them so you can evaluate how many of these signs and situations are pertinent to your loved one.

Signs

The person talks about suicide. The talk may seem to be in jest at first, but it persists. The person talks about "not being around anymore," or reflects on the time "when I'm gone," or comes right out and says, "I don't think I can go on anymore." When you hear this kind of talk, take the hint and ask (in as sympathetic and unintimidated a tone as you can muster) whether the person is thinking of committing suicide. Then be willing to sit down and engage in more lengthy dialogue, in a caring way. At worst, you may feel embarrassed when the person says that he or she is not talking about suicide and that you shouldn't worry. At best, you will start a process that might help save a life. More likely, you will simply show that you care, and this will be of help in and of itself, even if the person's mood is not serious.

The person makes "final plans." This may involve the writing a good-bye note, drawing up a will, taking out a life insurance policy on the spur of the moment, giving sentimental possessions away, and other manifestations of "getting one's affairs in order." Again, communication is a key intervention. Have the courage to ask the person directly why he or she is making such plans. If the person denies that anything is wrong, come right out and say that it looks as if he or she is preparing to die. Then be willing to discuss the matter at length.

The person's behavioral patterns change in disturbing ways. For example, a previously gregarious person begins to isolate himself or herself. Or, the person's moods change, with irritability, sadness, and apathy becoming more predominant. Of course, these may be signs of drug or alcohol abuse, or other emotional disturbances, and may not entail suicidality. However, since these problems sometimes coexist with (or are early warning signs of) suicidality, it is important to note these sorts of behavioral changes.

The person behaves in ways that are self-injurious or seem to invite danger and harm. This may involve driving recklessly, abusing substances, associating with dangerous people, disregarding his or her medical health (for example, neglecting to take insulin), and being cavalier about safety. Again, these behaviors are often associated with problems other than suicidality.

However, if such behaviors represent a marked departure from the way the person usually acts and are accompanied by comments such as "I don't really care what happens to me anyway" or "Who cares if I die?" it would be prudent for you to consider the possibility that this person is suicidal.

Situations

The person has experienced significant losses in a short period of time. In this case, he or she may be vulnerable to severe depression and perhaps suicidality. This is especially true if the losses have to do with the person's sense of identity and self-worth (for example, losing a career path unexpectedly) and the sense of meaningful connection to other people (for example, the death of a spouse). A tragic illustration of this phenomenon can be found in the case of a young woman at the University of Pennsylvania who took her own life in the months following her boyfriend's murder. Her suicide note indicated that she could not bear to go on without him.

The person suffers from a chronic illness. A person who is medically ill, experiences constant physical pain, and believes (rightly or wrongly) that the illness or condition will never get better is at increased risk for suicide. The combination of ceaseless pain with a sense of hopelessness is a very serious condition. In such cases, it is critical to offer realistic support and hope and to help with the provision of appropriate pain management.

The person has suffered extreme social humiliation. We have seen persons become suicidal in the aftermath of such events as a high-profile bankruptcy (splashed all over the business section of the local newspaper), public accusations of professional misconduct, or their family's discovery that they are homosexual.

The person abuses mind-altering substances and has access to firearms. Certain situations, in and of themselves, do not necessarily bring about a person's suicidality. However, their presence in the suicidal person's life makes the risk that much greater. The abuse of mind-altering substances such as alcohol, illicit drugs, and prescription painkillers, as well as the possession of firearms are two examples. It is routine procedure when treating a suicidal individual to assess whether the person has easy access to drugs or weapons and to take all reasonable steps to remove these instruments of self-destruction from the hands of a deeply depressed person.

Is This My Fault?

When you become aware that someone you love is contemplating taking his or her own life, you will naturally be concerned and scared. You may also feel guilty, wondering what you may have done to cause this, or what you have failed to do to prevent it. While this might be an understandable reaction to an extreme situation, it is useless to think that you are to blame.

Many factors come together to cause a person to consider suicide, as we have discussed throughout this book. To try to assess personal responsibility and blame likely will yield little insight or practical benefit, either for the person who feels guilty or the person who is suicidal. At the very least, blaming yourself will be a waste of time and energy at a moment when you need to summon up all the strength you've got. At worst, you will render yourself depressed as well, and you will be less apt to be of help in the days ahead, when the suicidal person may need your support and presence most of all. In absolute worst-case scenarios, we have seen people become suicidal themselves over a loved one's suicidality. Nobody benefits from this state of affairs.

What should you do if someone else blames you? This is a very painful situation, especially if it is the suicidal person who is holding you responsible for the suicidal feelings or attempt. Your first reaction might be extreme, either buying into the notion that it's all your fault or feeling unjustly accused and indignant and possibly responding with anger.

Extreme reactions like these are to be avoided whenever possible. Therefore, we suggest a middle-ground approach—do your best to ignore the entire issue of who is to blame, while you make yourself available to be as much help to your suicidal loved one as can be reasonably expected. If someone blames you, a good response might be, "That's neither here nor there. Right now, my main concern is [the suicidal persons] well-being." If the other person retorts, "You should have thought of that before," you can reply, "We'll never know for sure what anyone could have done, but right now I'm determined to help as much as I can." In other words, don't get backed into a defensive posture. Remain a levelheaded, caring problem solver, if possible.

She's Threatening to Kill Herself: What Should I Do?

The rule of thumb here is to seek middle ground between under- and over reacting. You should neither ignore the threat, hoping that it will go away, nor become agitated and overwrought. A serious, levelheaded demeanor is most helpful at this time.

In addition, we strongly suggest that you attempt to engage in dialogue with the person who is making the suicidal threat. Some people think that talking never solves anything, but we completely disagree. While it may be true that a single conversation is not a panacea for all major problems, it does serve a number of valuable functions. It helps to make a connection with a person who otherwise may be trying to *disconnect* from life. A conversation also gives you the opportunity to provide the suicidal person with a new perspective.

For example, "Lanny" became suicidal when he was not accepted into medical school. He believed that his father would be ashamed of him, and the young man became convinced that his life was worthless. By talking with him, his father convinced Lanny that he was not ashamed of him and that, in fact, he was proud of his son in many respects. This offered the young man a perspective he had not been able to gain on his own, and his sense of desperation abated, even though he remained understandably disappointed.

Communicating with the suicidal person also stimulates thinking and reasoning. People who are depressed and hopeless often evidence thinking patterns that are negatively biased. They show a lack of reasoned thinking, and they often act primarily on their emotions. When it's a matter of life and death, as it is in cases of suicidality, it is imperative that the suicidal person be encouraged and stimulated into thinking things through. A conversation helps this process significantly.

What if the suicidal individual possesses the means to kill himself or herself and threatens to use it? If your loved one is not actively wielding a weapon or a bottle of pills, you can take your time and try to negotiate the surrender of these instruments of potential suicide. Make a strong point that your loved one should not have the means by which to die on the spur of the moment, but don't be so heavy-handed that it makes the other person defensive or combative. Show respect for the other person's point of view, and for his or her right to make an autonomous decision, even as you make a plea for that person to consider another way. Do what you can to make the relinquishing of pills, poisons, or weapons a collaborative process. This makes it possible for the suicidal person to have an active say in his or her own decision to live, which is a more secure and enduring state of affairs than the coercive alternative.

We understand that, at times, it may be necessary for you to make a decision for the suicidal person, but no human being can do this forever. No matter how good your intentions are, and no matter how vigilant you are in watching over the suicidal person like a hawk, you cannot be a guardian angel 24 hours a day, 7 days a week, for all of your life. At some point, it will be necessary to rely on your loved one's acceptance of life, and rejection of suicide. The other person's life is not solely your responsibility. This fact is often difficult and scary to accept. We want to do everything we can to help our loved ones to overcome crises and get on with their lives, and sometimes we can make a difference for the better. In the end, however, the decision to live or to commit suicide lies with the individual.

Finally, you should not try to face the crisis of a suicidal loved one alone. Other people need to know, so that they may offer assistance. Sometimes these "others" are friends or family members. More often, they are professionals. For example, if your loved one calls to tell you that he or she has just taken an entire bottle of medication, you will need to call for an ambulance right away. Before you call for the paramedics, ask the suicidal person the following questions, and try to keep your head about you enough to take coherent notes:

- Where are you? (address, if possible)

- What action have you taken to harm yourself?

- (If applicable) What substance have you ingested, and how much?

- How long ago did you do this?

- Can you hold while I make a call? (or) Can I call you right back after I call for help? I want to talk to you until the ambulance gets there.

There is no guarantee that the person will give you this information, but it is most prudent for you to make an attempt to get these facts as quickly as possible so that you can communicate meaningful information to the professionals who will soon be attending to your loved one.

Other ways of enlisting the help of professionals is facilitating the suicidal person's involvement in psychotherapy (and perhaps medication treatment as well) and (in more immediately serious instances) admission to a hospital. *Never make therapy or hospitalization sound like a threat or punishment.* The purpose of treatment is to protect, preserve, and improve the life of your loved one. It is decidedly not to take away his or her freedom, to "dump" him or her on someone else, or to win an interpersonal power struggle.

One way to make this point effectively is to volunteer (to both the suicidal person and the professional in charge of his or her therapy) your appropriate involvement in the treatment. What constitutes "appropriate" involvement will vary, but it can range from daily visits, to taking part in couple's or family therapy, to monitoring the person's compliance with medications, to getting individual professional help yourself (for example, when you need to learn to cope more effectively with the loved one's behavior at home).

What Can I Do if He Refuses to Be Helped?

Few things in life are more frustrating than knowing that a loved one is in serious trouble, watching his or her life deteriorate, and feeling as if you've tried everything but there is nothing you can do about it. One example of this scenario is when you suspect that someone you care for is deeply depressed, but the person denies it, rejects all forms of help, and simply asks that you "go away and leave me alone."

If your attempts to help are rebuffed, do not automatically assume that your demonstrations of caring and concern are wholly unwelcome. We have noted that individuals who are considering suicide often are ambivalent, even when their words or behaviors suggest otherwise. Therefore, although the suicidal person may bristle outwardly in response to your expressions of worry, he or she also may be silently noting that you extended yourself in a kind way. If you express your concerns compassionately and make your suggestions about "getting some professional help" respectfully, the suicidal person will probably mull over what you have said, even though he or she may not accept your comments right away. Later, at their own behest, and of their own accord, suicidal persons may decide to seek and accept help. The key here is to allow the individual the autonomy and self-respect to draw his or her own conclusions, without feeling as if he or she is being coerced or "committed."

If you are closely related to, or involved with, a suicidal person who does not want to get into treatment, you are undoubtedly feeling a great strain. In such instances, it is often a good idea to seek counseling of your own, much in the same way that the spouse of a problem drinker can attend Al-Anon meetings. You may choose to find a support group, join a general therapy group, or commence individual therapy. First and foremost, do this for yourself, because your well-being is important, too. If your suicidal loved one is truly rejecting all your attempts to help, over a long period of time, there is no law that says you have to suffer along in silence and solitude. You need to be able to live your own life as best you can and get validation and support for this.

There is an additional benefit that sometimes occurs when the non-suicidal significant other or relative starts a course of therapy. The suicidal person may join the process. By going into therapy yourself, you show in a powerful way that you do not believe that being a patient is something to be ashamed of. You show that you are serious about your worries, and that you are willing to look at your own role in the relationship and in the suicidality of the loved one. You will be modeling the appropriate ways to seeks help for a serious problem that seems overwhelming and out of control. To some extent, you will be helping the suicidal loved one to save face, because you will have been the one who sought treatment first. Remember, if you are going to seek counseling on your own, it is vital that you do so primarily for yourself. However, if it leads the suicidal person to seek help too, then you will have taken two important steps.

As a last resort, there are times when you can compel your suicidal loved one to get professional help if he or she will not follow through voluntarily. We are talking about the situation when you may have to commit the suicidal person involuntarily into a hospital. We understand that this is an unpleasant process, and that is why we call it the last resort. In fact, it is often not legally possible to do this at all, because most statutes demand that the person be shown to be openly dangerous to themselves or others. Constant verbal threats of suicide are insufficient in and of themselves.

The most practical and humane time to consider involuntary hospitalization for your loved one is in the aftermath of a serious self-harming incident. Such occurrences, including overdosing, cutting the wrists, and poisoning by gas, usually lead to emergency medical care in a hospital. When this happens, hospital personnel often will begin the commitment process themselves. However, you can play a major role in making this procedure go more smoothly by providing the professional staff with information, cooperating with them, and helping your suicidal loved one to deal with the situation. You will continue to be of significant assistance if you play an active role in the suicidal person's care and if you are a positive presence during your hospital visits.

In a perfect world, involuntary hospitalization would never be needed—everyone who needed help would seek it freely on his or her own. Given that we live in the real world, you may need to take this unpopular step in order to provide the suicidal individual with the medical treatment and supervision he or she needs. Hospitalization is not a panacea, and it does not substitute for long-term solutions to the problems of depression and suicidality, but it can save a life at a particularly critical time.

What Do I Do if I Feel I'm Being Manipulated by the Suicide Threats?

A very tricky and troublesome situation arises when you believe you are being manipulated by the suicide threats of another person. When we say "manipulated," we mean that the suicide threat appears to be an attempt to scare you or play on possible guilty feelings to make you do something you believe is unhealthy, counterproductive, against your better judgment, or otherwise contrary to your first instinct. Further, this scenario takes place repeatedly, and begins to cast doubt on the validity of the other person's claim that he or she has no agenda other than truly wanting to die.

Meanwhile, your sympathy and concern begin to dissolve into anger and resentment. You feel trapped in a situation over which you cannot gain adequate control, because the stakes are too high to ignore, so you believe you cannot disregard the threat. This is especially the case when the suicidal person frequently makes self-harming gestures (for example, superficial wrist cuts, "mini-overdoses," etc.) in the aftermath of disagreements with you. As a result, the sense of collaboration and togetherness you once had with the suicidal person diminishes significantly, while the uncomfortable power struggle increases.

What can you do about this? We'll begin with a discussion about what *not* to do. Do not get into an argument with the suicidal person about whether or not he or she is really serious about wanting to die. It is understandable that you may want to vent in this manner, but such a confrontation rarely serves a constructive function. If the person making the suicide threats is at all ambivalent about life and death—that is, if he or she even has an inkling that suicide is a viable option—your argument likely will be interpreted as a callous miscalculation, and the relationship will be strained further. In addition, the suicidal person may then escalate the suicidal threats and gestures in order to "prove" that you were wrong. This can lead to an increase in lethality. Your guilt and anger will increase proportionally, and the power struggle will intensify, to no one's benefit.

You may also be tempted to confront the suicidal person with the idea that he or she is deliberately manipulating you. Arguably, there may be times when this is necessary and perhaps even helpful. However, those times are few and far between. For example, such a confrontation may best be presented within the confines of a joint therapy session, but not in everyday life. Given that it is rarely useful to say, "You're being manipulative," to a person who is threatening suicide, what else *can* you do?

Continue to make it clear to the suicidal person that you do not want him or her to die. Spell out the fact that you wish to be helpful, in whatever reasonable way possible, and that you wish for the suicidal person to recover from his or her deep depression so that he or she may have a happier life. At the same time, do not do things against your will in order to "prove" that you really care and want to help. Your words and sincere actions will have to suffice, for the sake of your well-being, as well as the long-term well-being of the suicidal person.

Clearly, this philosophy and strategy are difficult. For example, how are you supposed to respond when someone says the following to you?

- If you really cared whether I lived or died, you'd quit your job and stay home with me.

- If you won't agree to continuing our romantic relationship, I'll kill myself, and it will be all your fault.

- If you don't stop nagging me to give up drinking, I'll have no choice but to kill myself to get it over with.

- You make me want to die.

These kinds of comments wreak havoc in relationships, because they feed into both parties' feelings of anger, frustration, and guilt. Notice what these statements have in common: *They make someone else's decision whether or not to commit suicide conditional on your responses.* In order to deal with this dilemma most effectively and fairly to all parties, you need to remind yourself that you are not threatening the other person with homicide. The other person is threatening suicide. If you clearly state that you wish the other no harm, but the individual continues to maintain that your actions are causing the problem, you are dealing with someone who needs immediate professional attention, much more so than they need your capitulation.

If you do give in to the suicidal person's demands, without at least also suggesting that he or she contact a therapist, it is likely that the same scenario will repeat itself again and again. As a result, nothing meaningful will have changed. You will still be angry, the suicidal person will still be at risk for self-harm at any time, and the issues causing the person's deep depression and desperate behaviors will not have been addressed in any meaningful way.

In sum, you can express your support and concern for the suicidal person *and* firmly maintain your position not to obey demands that go against your better judgment or wishes. You can do *both*, notwithstanding the suicidal individual's protestations to the contrary. We realize you will have to use your own words, and your situations may be different from the ones on which we focus, but we would like to share with you some sample responses to the suicidal comments listed earlier.

- The fact that I love you and I am concerned about you is already beyond doubt. I have proven myself time and time again, and I do not believe that I need to continue to prove myself. I want to be with you, but I will not quit my job. I think we can spare your life without sacrificing our livelihood in the process. The fact is, you need more help and attention than any one person can give you. Therefore, the answer is not that I quit my job, but rather that we get you more intensive treatment.

- I am not discontinuing our relationship to be cruel or to cause you pain. I am very, very sorry if you are hurt. I wish only the best for you in the future, but I will not be a part of it. Your life's worth should be based on more than just being in a relationship with me. Even if I were to stay with you, it would not solve our problems. In fact, to be in a relationship in which you cannot live without the other person, and in which the other person is frightened into staying, is not the basis for a healthy relationship, and I think you know that. I want you to live and to be happy, but you will have to find that without me.

- The reason I keep telling you that you need help for your drinking problem is that I already believe you are killing yourself slowly, and I do not want that to happen. It makes little sense for me to ignore the problem of your drinking yourself to death, out of fear that you might kill yourself if I bother you too much. I guess what this points out is that you have to be responsible for your own behavior, and I have to get into Al-Anon.

- I am not sure what you are trying to accomplish by telling me that I "make you want to die,"—and I am not in a position to tell you what you are feeling and what you are not feeling—but I *can* tell you that I don't want you to die, and I am not trying to cause you any pain. I really don't know why you feel the way you do, but it bears no resemblance to what I am feeling.

These statements are examples of ways to steer around feelings of manipulation in your relationship with a suicidal individual. Such comments often will not be received favorably, and the interpersonal struggle may escalate unless you keep your cool and continue to express your concern, without having to stand on your head to prove something. Hang in there, be assertive, be compassionate, and progress might follow.

What Should I Be Careful *Not* to Do?

Here we discuss the six most common mistakes concerned others make to help you become aware of what to avoid when dealing with a suicidal person.

Mistake 1: Saying nothing at all, because you are afraid that if you bring up the topic of suicide you will "put the idea into the person's head" or "push them over the edge." There is no evidence that you can make a nonsuicidal person suicidal simply by raising the issue in a concerned way. Neither can you make a person who is pondering a decision about life and death summarily choose death just because you offered kind and caring words about his or her well-being. If anything, you will pave the way for the suicidal person to feel accepted and perhaps to agree to get desperately needed professional help. By opening up the lines of communication, you show that you notice their pain, that they matter to you, and that there is hope.

Mistake 2: Assuming that if suicidal persons "really" wanted to commit suicide, they would "just do it"; therefore, if they talk about it, they must not really be serious. In actuality, the majority of people who are dangerously suicidal are *ambivalent* about taking such a plunge into the eternal unknown. They are weighing the question, "To be or not to be?" heavily in their minds, and it is natural for them to bounce this question off other people in the course of this most serious deliberation. When they do this, *take it at face value and do not minimize it*. If you dismiss it, you may raise the level of risk because you will have cut off serious and substantive communication between yourself and your loved one.

Further, since deeply depressed persons tend to be highly sensitive to personal rejection, you may inadvertently give the impression that you don't care how they feel or whether they live or die. This is not the message that you want to send at such a critical time. By contrast, open and accepting communication is vital. This lowers the risk.

Mistake 3: Telling suicidal persons that they are being silly because they have "so much to live for." Even if you are objectively correct—that in a healthy state of mind the suicidal person would realize that he or she has a great deal to live for—it is categorically *not* silly for a depressed person to lose objectivity and to feel such subjective pain that nothing else seems to matter. In some instances, suicidal persons will actually become more discouraged by such a comment. They may either conclude that you didn't even try to understand or become more self-reproachful for feeling suicidal even when things are going well (expressed by, "I'm so ungrateful for the things I have. This just proves that I deserve to die").

If you can try to comprehend the suicidal person's point of view first, you will avoid coming across as patronizing, and you will succeed in demonstrating that you have warmth and respect for the individual. The act of caring and listening will in and of itself be tangible evidence that there is indeed something to live for, though it may take time, additional support from loved ones, professional help, and perhaps medication before the suicidal person realizes the fuller range of benefits of continuing to live.

Mistake 4: Assuming that once an acute suicidal crisis is over, everything is back to normal, and nobody has to be concerned with the suicidal person anymore. This is understandable but wishful thinking. It is extremely painful to watch a friend or relative in the throes of despair, and it is terribly worrisome to face the risk of losing that person to a sudden, tragic, premature death.

Naturally, once such a crisis subsides, we have a strong tendency to forget all about such painful matters and to put it all behind us. We would like to think that it was just a phase that the suicidal person was going through. The more common reality is that there are substantial reasons for a person becoming suicidal in the first place; reasons that are not likely to go away for good overnight. Unless these reasons are dealt with thoroughly, it is likely that the person will evidence recurrent bouts of depression and suicidality, especially when he or she goes through periods of transition or stress (for example, moving to a new geographical location, switching careers, splitting up with a love partner, or having a baby). In order to reduce this likelihood, the suicidal person must have a forum—perhaps a therapist's office—to explore and take stock of what brought him or her to such a point of desperation, even after the acute crisis is over.

Mistake 5: Telling the suicidal person to "snap out of it" or using the prospect of getting professional help as a threat, rather than as a hopeful, appropriate, nonstigmatized option. Sometimes people have the mistaken notion that they can shame or coerce someone into "snapping out of it" and that they can the hold the trump card of therapy or hospitalization as a scare tactic to dissuade the suicidal person from making gestures or otherwise acting out.

This is unwise for a number of reasons. First, telling someone the equivalent of "just get over it or you're going to have to go where the nut cases go" is oversimplistic, unsympathetic, inattentive to the substantive problems that need to be addressed, and unconducive to ongoing communication. Second, it reinforces the notion that needing professional help warrants a scarlet letter (C for *crazy*) and therefore discourages the suicidal person from seeking treatment. Third, it demonstrates a disparaging attitude toward the suicidal person, which may further damage the individual's already low self-esteem. Fourth, it punishes the person's attempt to elicit help and therefore may encourage him or her to withdraw to a point where nobody has the opportunity to help. Finally, using the prospect of professional help as a threat may scare off suicidal persons who might otherwise have sought help. Instead, they may come to view therapy as a loss of freedom, an abdication of control over their life, and a general detriment to their well-being. It gives the impression that you either take a dim view of therapy yourself or see it as being useful only insofar as it deprives the suicidal person of his or her autonomy.

Mistake 6: Giving in to your exasperation by saying, "If you're going to kill yourself, just go ahead and get it over with already, and stop tormenting me with your incessant threats!" This is the sort of comment that you might say in the heat of argument or when your guard is down. You must strive never to make such an inflammatory statement to a person who may be suicidal. It may relieve your frustration temporarily, but it will probably compound your stress in the long run, owing to the almost certain adverse effect that it will have on the other person, which may escalate his or her suicidality and threats.

Whether or not this type of provocative exclamation precipitates the other person's making an actual suicide attempt, it will at the very least be indelibly etched in the suicidal individual's memory that you "wished" him or her to be dead. This will damage a relationship that might otherwise be less conflicted and contentious.

When you find yourself on the receiving end of an angry, depressed person's spouting a litany of suicide threats, that is the time simply to recommend that a professional be consulted, and to add, "I want to help you, but it's beyond my ability to do so. Your depression is too deep for me to know how to handle it. I care about you and I don't want you to die, but it's distressing for me to hear you talk about suicide so often. I'll support you in whatever way I can, but right now you need to make an appointment with a therapist."

If you're so exasperated that you find it difficult to summon up restraint and diplomacy, a concerned silence may be a useful alternative—one of the few times that a lack of words is a suitable form of communication. Later, when you've had the chance to calm down, you may be able to adopt the tone of the words above. If you find yourself blurting out comments that you quickly regret, *it's never too late to apologize*, and to remind the suicidal person of your care and concern.

B

Resources

Books

Your Perfect Right: A Guide to Assertive Living (6th ed.), by Robert E. Alberti and Michael L. Emmons. San Luis Obispo, CA: Impact, 1990.

The Relaxation Response, by Herbert Benson. New York: William Morrow, 1975.

The Feeling Good Handbook, by David Burns. Plume 1989.

Stronger Than Death: When Suicide Touches Your Life, by Sue Chance. Avon, 1994.

The Depression Workbook: A Guide for Living with Depression and Manic Depression, by Mary Ellen Copeland. New Harbinger, 1992.

The Relaxation & Stress Reduction Workbook (4th ed.), by Martha Davis, Elizabeth Eshelman, and Matthew McKay. Oakland, CA: New Harbinger Publications, 1995.

How to Stubbornly Refuse to Make Yourself Miserable about Anything, Yes Anything! by Albert Ellis. Lyle Stuart, 1988.

Man's Search for Meaning, by Victor Frankl. Pocket Books, 1959.

When Living Hurts: For Teenagers and Young Adults, by Sol Gordon. Union of American Hebrew Congregationalists, 1985.

Wherever You Go, There You Are, by Jon Kabat-Zinn. Delacorte Press, 1993.

14,000 Things to be Happy About, by Barbara Ann Kipfer. New York: Workman Publishing, 1990.

Overcoming Depression, by Paul Hauck. Westminster John Knox, 1973.

In The Mind's Eye: The Power Of Imagery For Personal Enrichment, by Arnold Lazarus. New York: Guilford, 1977.

Questions and Answers about Suicide, by David Lester. Charles Press, 1989.

I Cant Get Over It: A Handbook for Trauma Survivors, by Aphrodite Matsakis. New Harbinger, 1992.

Prisoners of Belief: Exposing and Changing Beliefs that Control Your Life, by Matthew McKay and Patrick Fanning. New Harbinger, 1991.

Healthy Pleasures, by Robert Ornstein and David Sobel. Addison-Wesley, 1989.

Suicide: The Forever Decision, by Paul G. Quinett. Continuum, 1987.

Anger: The Misunderstood Emotion, by Carol Tavris. New York: Touchstone Books, 1989.

Organizations

American Association of Suicidology
    4201 Connecticut Avenue, NW, Suite 310
    Washington, DC 20008
    (202) 237-2280

Suicide Education and Information Centre
    201-1615-10th Ave., SW
    Calgary, AB Canada
    T3C 0J7
    (403) 245-3900

Internet Sites

American Association of Suicidology
    http://www.cyberpsych.org/aas.htm

Suicide Awareness/Voices of Education
    http://www.save.org

Depression Central
    http://www.psycom.net/depression.central.html

The Grohol Mental Health Page
    http://csbh.mhv.net/%7Egrohol/

References

Beck, A. T. 1967. *Depression: Clinical, Experimental, and Theoretical Aspects.* New York: Harper & Row.

Beck, A. T., Rush, A. J., Shaw, B. F., and Emery, G. 1979. *Cognitive Therapy of Depression.* New York: Guilford.

Ellis, A. 1988. *How to Refuse to Make Yourself Miserable About Anything . . . Yes, Anything!* Seacaucus, NJ: Lyle Stuart.

Ellis, A. 1994. *Reason and Emotion in Psychotherapy: A Comprehensive Method of Treating Human Disturbances.* 2d ed. New York: Birch Lane Press.

Ellis, A. and Harper, R. A. 1975. *A New Guide to Rational Living.* North Hollywood, CA: Wilshire Books.

Ellis, T. E. 1986. "Toward a Cognitive Therapy for Suicidal Individuals." *Professional Psychology: Research and Practice* 17: 125–130.

Ellis, T. E. 1987. "A Cognitive Approach to Treating the Suicidal Client." In *Innovations in Clinical Practice,* ed. P. Keller and S. Heyman, vol. 5, 93–107. Sarasota, FL: Professional Resource Exchange.

Freeman, A. and Reinecke, M. 1993. *Cognitive Therapy of Suicidal Behavior: A Manual for Treatment.* New York: Springer.

Fremouw, W. J., dePerczel, M., and Ellis, T. E. 1990. *Suicide Risk: Assessment and Response Guidelines.* New York: Allyn & Bacon.

Layden, M. A., Newman, C. F., Freeman, A., and Morse, S. B. 1993. *Cognitive Therapy of Borderline Personality Disorder.* Needham Heights, MA: Allyn & Bacon.

Linehan, M. 1993. *Cognitive-Behavioral Treatment of Borderline Personality Disorder.* New York: Guilford.

Vaillant, G. E. 1977. *Adaptation to Life.* Boston: Little Brown.

Wolpe, J. 1982. *The Practice of Behavior Therapy.* 3d ed. New York: Pergamon.

Index

Pages on which charts and figures appear in this book are italicized below.

Other New Harbinger Self-Help Titles